TWO TOURS

Viet Nam at War - Viet Nam in Peace

Harry F. Thomas

This book is dedicated to my wife, Lauren. She saved all the letters I wrote her while I was in the Viet Nam War allowing me to recall many of my experiences during my time there. She also lovingly steered me toward a prosperous post war career. We share many memories of the Viet Nam era.

CONTENTS

PART I - Youth, War and Change

ACKNOWLEDGEMENTS

I'm most grateful to my friend and gifted piano teacher John Boyajy for his meticulous editing of this book's manuscript. In search of perfection, he applied the same principles that he uses in teaching and playing the piano, and the results significantly improved the readability of my book. Thank you also to my friends who read the first draft and encouraged me to publish my book.

FORWARD

This book was written in the hope that I might pass my knowledge and wisdom, especially that which I gained from my time in the Viet Nam War, to the young people I love. Perhaps they might absorb wisdom and understanding without the pain of the actual experience. Secondly, I wrote in an attempt to provide a brief history of American involvement in the war. When I returned to Viet Nam in 2012, one of my fellow tourists, someone my age, asked me, "How did we get involved here anyway?" It was, for me, a hurtful and piercing question. The Prologue contains a brief history. I've added my own perspective of the context in which America viewed the world as it moved into the war. Thirdly, I wrote to chronicle my experiences observing the growing failures of the United States government and its military forces to subdue the lesser equipped rebels and army of a small third world country. I was in Viet Nam for the Tet Offensive, the political turning point of the war. Part I of this book chronicles my wartime experiences and perspective, my pain, my confusion and my growing sense of disbelief in what was happening. Finally, I wrote to solidify my understanding of the war and my conclusions regarding its outcome and effect. Part II chronicles my return to Viet Nam thirty-seven years after the war ended in an effort to find my personal peace.

When I was in Viet Nam I did not slosh through the jungles on point as depicted in the movies. I did not take part in special offensives or in any particular battles. I never fired a shot at the enemy. I did nothing heroic and I often wonder if what I did made any difference at all. Nevertheless, my experiences and those of tens of thousands of other soldiers who were not in direct combat were often intense, life-threatening, life-changing and worthy of being chronicled. In the Viet Nam War old concepts of the front line and the rear were blurred and perhaps lost forever. Enemy forays and attacks were launched at almost every American military unit in the country regardless of the unit's role.

Those who experience war and return are changed, sometimes physically but always emotionally. My grandfather returned from World War I shell-shocked. Although he became a successful contractor, he was never as psychologically stable as he had been before the war. My uncle was captured by the German Army during World War II and was held as a prisoner of war. He returned and carried the deep memorable scars of war for the balance of his life. My father and my other uncles returned from World War II without apparent physical or mental injuries, but as I talked with them I found that their wartime experiences had changed their lives in a myriad of ways. My grandfather, father and uncles became men while in war. Their change from boyhood to manhood would have occurred without war, but war accelerated the change and thrust foreign pigments into the dyes cast to form their adulthood at the very time of their coming of age. The colors of their adulthood became deeply forged into their being, blended and woven into soft, often hidden, pastels in some parts and decisive, strong acrylics in others. Parts of their persona; those experiences of fear, terror, loss and camaraderie; remained obscured; rarely shared and only understood by others who went to war. Those who returned from Viet Nam felt that sense of isolation with even greater intensity.

My relatives went to war with mixed amounts of patriotism, fear, adventure and familial sadness. Drafted or not, they went willingly, driven by a sense of duty and the social belief that what they were doing was the right thing to do. In the mid-1960s it came to pass that I and my generation, a cross-section of the youth of working-class of America, were called to war in Viet Nam. We went, as had our grandfathers, fathers and uncles, with a sense of duty. We too went at the time of our coming of age and we too returned as indelibly changed men. The wars of our antecedents were declared wars that lasted three or four years and were supported by a majority of the government, the people and the press. Our elders returned generally satisfied that they had performed their duty. Most of them retained their faith in the wisdom of their country to make the decisions of war and peace. The Viet Nam War lasted for nearly eleven years. It was not a declared war and it never garnered a majority of public, government or media support. We returned from war as men, independently and one at a time, changed not only by our maturation, but also - unlike its predecessors - by the particular dissonance of the Viet Nam War.

Unlike the veterans of the wars of our elders, many Viet Nam War Veterans carry a tiny piece of shrapnel deep inside that will forever tease at the question: Did we and our country do the right thing? In 2012 I returned to Viet Nam with my family, in part to answer that question.

A note: I have opted to use "Viet Nam", the Vietnamese language name, rather than the western "Vietnam" throughout this book.

Harry Thomas – Novato, California 2012

NORTH
VIETNAM

DMZ

Da Nang
Hoi An

LAOS

THAILAND

I CORPS

Qui Nhon

II CORPS

SOUTH

CHINA

SEA

CAMBODIA

III CORPS

Saigon

IV
CORPS

GULF
OF SIAM

PROLOGUE - BUILD UP AND WAR

In the years after my wartime experience, I have read extensively about America's military involvement and the escalation of the war in Viet Nam. I've studied hard in my attempt to try and understand how my fellow soldiers and I wound up there, some to return and some to die. I've decided that America's involvement in Viet Nam was based on misunderstanding and fear. America feared communism and held a heavily biased perception of the world's politics as they existed after World War II. Although fear and misunderstanding may be the essence and generalized cause of the Viet Nam war, the politics and events leading up to it were far more complicated.

Several times in the world's history one war has set the stage for another. World War II set the stage for the Viet Nam War. Before World War II began French colonialists occupied Viet Nam. The French, like the Dutch, English, Germans and Portuguese, profited economically through their trade and governance of the territories they possessed. Although the people they governed seemed content, in the grand scheme of things many were not, and occasional rebellion was common. This was true in the French colony of Viet Nam, one of the three countries (including Cambodia and Laos) sharing common boarders that comprised what was known as French Indochina.

The Japanese invaded Viet Nam at the beginning of the Second World War and they overtook the country while the French fought to defend their country from the Germans. France fell to the Germans and Vietnam fell to the Japanese. Some French citizens, sympathetic to the Germans, established a wartime French government. Named after its headquarters in Vichy, it was a puppet of the Germans and was sympathetic to their Japanese allies. The Japanese occupying Viet Nam partnered with the French Vichy government and together they cruelly occupied and ruled Viet Nam and its people.

The cruelty of the Vichy French-Japanese occupation created significant underground opposition in Viet Nam. This opposition became manifest through the actions of the Viet Minh, a military force organized by Ho Chi Minh to fight and oppose the Japanese. Ho was a Vietnamese patriot who had traveled and studied extensively throughout the world. He was also a proponent of the communist/socialist ideas of Marx and Lenin.

Ho Chi Minh's Viet Minh army used guerilla tactics to fight against the Japanese and Vichy French. Ho chose Vo Nguyen Giap, a former history professor, as his general to lead the Viet Minh. Giap later became the general that thoroughly frustrated the United Stated during the Viet Nam War some twenty-five years later.

The Axis powers (Japan, Germany and Italy) waged war against the United States, France, England and Russia. The United States and its western allies supported Ho Chi Minh and the Viet Minh in their efforts to fight the Japanese in Viet Nam. This support included money, advice, and armaments.

With help from Ho Chi Minh, Western allied forces pushed the Japanese out of Viet Nam at the end of the war. This left a political vacuum. There was a brief effort to form a provisional Vietnamese government, but it failed and the pre-war French returned to control the country. Having fought the Japanese on behalf of the people of Viet Nam, Ho Chi Minh remained a force in support of, and in hope for a free Viet Nam. His Viet Minh were still intact and led by General Giap, and they were not interested in having their country reoccupied by a foreign government. Ho, Giap and the Viet Minh turned their guerilla war tactics against the returned French. The French battled the insurgent Viet Minh from 1946 until 1954 in what was called the First Indochina War. In an ironic twist, The United States, a former supporter of Ho Chi Minh against the Japanese, and now a former World War II ally of the French, supported the French in their efforts to rid Viet Nam of Ho Chi Minh and the Viet Minh. In spite of U.S. support, General Giap defeated the French in 1954 at the battle of Dien Bien Phu.

While the Viet Minh fought the French in Viet Nam, the rest of the world struggled through a plethora of confusing post-World War II events primary among them being the rise of communist Russia (The U.S.S.R.) and what came to be called the Cold War. Russia gained control of Eastern Europe and imposed its authoritarian communist government upon the nations of that area. Additionally, the democratic leaders of China, another country invaded by the Japanese in World War II, were forced out of that country. Chiang Kai-Shek, China's democratic leader during World War II, and his government fled China under the advancing Chinese communists led by Mao Tse-tung. In 1950 North Korea, another communist country, invaded South Korea and began the three-year-long Korean War. Korea was backed by Communist China. Such events created serious concerns on the part of the United States and its western allies who feared that the spread of communism would threaten the world's security.

In 1953 the Soviet Union, a communist country, exploded its first hydrogen bomb. It appeared to the U.S. and the west that communists armed with nuclear weapons were taking over as much of the world as possible in a direct challenge to western democracy and capitalism. Driven by this fear, and thinking that Ho Chi Minh and his Viet Minh were communists, the United States supported the French against Ho Chi Minh. Despite U.S. and Western support, the Viet Minh had defeated the French. The **Western world observed this defeat by what appeared to be a communist army and panicked.** The West immediately bargained for a settlement.

The settlement was reflected in the Geneva Accords of 1954. The Accords partitioned Viet Nam at the 17th parallel. Ho Chi Minh and the Viet Minh retained control of the North while the West selected a Vietnamese politician named Bao Dai to head a quickly established non-communist government in the south. Before World War II, Bao Dai had been Viet Nam's French-backed figurehead emperor. South Viet Nam under Bao Dai remained part of the French Union. The Accords called for a nationwide free election to be held in 1956.

Free elections, however, never took place because South Viet Nam withdrew from the French Union and became a sovereign state. Bao Dai, who performed poorly and was known for considerable corruption, was deposed in favor of Ngo Dinh Diem. Diem, an anti-communist catholic, became president with the backing of the United States. Some historians suspect that the support of Diem in the south and the failed elections, as called for in the Geneva Accords, were the West's way of avoiding the likely election of Ho Chi Minh whose popularity was widespread in the north *and* the south. Indeed many in the south viewed Bao Dai and Ngo Dinh Diem as corrupt, upper-class politicians with little interest in the welfare of the average Vietnamese.

The south, under Diem, became the Republic of South Vietnam, and received significant financial, political and other support from the United States and the West. Ho Chi Minh governed North Viet Nam and received financial, political and other backing from Communist China and the Union of Soviet Socialist Republics. A true polarized split of communist north vs. non-communist south resulted.

Meanwhile, the Cold War between the West and the U.S.S.R. increased in intensity. Concerned with the possible spread of communism, U.S. President Eisenhower pledged his full support to the Republic of South Viet Nam and its president, Diem. Most unfortunately, however, Diem ran a ruthless and corrupt government and did not tolerate dissent. His dictatorial behavior and obvious corruption created considerable opposition: unhappy poorer people in the south who joined forces with the Viet Minh and began fighting back against Diem's regime. By the end of the 1950s open firefights occurred between Diem's Republic of Viet Nam troops and the opposing Viet Minh and their southern sympathizers. Many of the southern forces opposing Diem claimed to be non-communist Vietnamese nationalists seeking to overthrow Diem and reunify Viet Nam. But Diem, a cunning politician, called his southern opposition the Viet Cong, meaning Viet Communists. That moniker soon reached the ears of the ever-fearful anti-communist West. The U.S. increased its support of Diem and began supplying him with additional funds, munitions and training for his troops.

John F. Kennedy succeeded Eisenhower and took office as president of the United States in January of 1961. During his presidency he and the United States experienced the frightening Cuban Missile Crisis of October 1962. The Soviet Union had installed nuclear missiles on the island of Cuba within easy range of the United States and the U.S. responded by blockading Soviet ships sent to supply the island. Diplomacy ended the crisis, but both nations came to the very brink of nuclear war. This crisis chilled the world and intensified the western world's fear of communists and communism.

In Viet Nam, the Viet Cong continued their guerilla war against the Diem regime, which prompted President Kennedy to send a team of American advisors to Viet Nam to help Diem to assess the situation. At the end of 1962 some 9,000 U.S. troops were stationed in the country.

In early November of 1963 President Diem was overthrown and killed in a coup by a group of his own generals. A few weeks later President Kennedy was assassinated. Diem was replaced by Ngo Dinh Nhu; an equally corrupt, anti-communist, upper-class politician. His step into power and his rampant anti-Buddhist actions further amplified the revolutionary activities of the Viet Cong and the poorer South Vietnamese classes. Kennedy's successor, Lyndon Johnson was not skilled at foreign policy and he reacted to the new situation in Viet Nam by increasing its U.S. military and economic support.

In August of 1964, U.S. naval destroyers patrolling off the coast of Viet Nam were allegedly attacked by Vietnamese torpedo boats. Reports of the attacks, occurring in the Gulf of Tonkin, were sketchy, and to this day a full understanding of the actual events remains unclear. As a result of the reports of the attacks, President Johnson asked Congress for a resolution allowing him to take any actions necessary to wage a conventional war against those forces opposing the Republic of South Viet Nam. Congress quickly passed the resolution, known as the Gulf of Tonkin Resolution. Johnson immediately exercised his new power and by the end of 1964 U.S. military strength in Viet Nam reached 23,000 personnel.

In October of 1964 Communist China successfully tested its first atomic bomb thereby increasing America's fear of communism. The west viewed the Viet Cong in Viet Nam as an arm of communist China *and* China had the bomb. The Viet Cong increased their guerilla warfare in South Viet Nam and President Johnson called for an additional build-up of American forces in the country. In May of 1965, members of the III Marine Amphibious Forces landed in Da Nang to defend the logistical support installations operating there (naval and air force operations). By June of 1965 American forces numbered 82,000. In July Johnson called for another 100,000, a request that made headlines in the nation's newspapers[1]. Johnson called for another 100,000 troops in 1966, the year I was drafted into the U.S. Army. By the end of 1967 American military strength in Viet Nam approached 500,000 and the United States was fully committed in Viet Nam. I was a part of that build-up of troops.

---

[1] These were the headlines my family and I viewed in the summer of 1965 at Arlington National Cemetery. See Chapter 1.

PART I

Youth, War and Change

CHAPTER 1 - PREMONITION

I'm a native Californian. My family dates back in California to the Gold Rush and in Marin County, where I was born, to 1852. I was raised in the 1950's and early sixties, a time of American unity, growth and prosperity. My family and my extended family were hard working, honest, patriotic, blue collar, and loving folks. My parent's generation had survived the great depression and World War II. They strived to live a peaceful family life and to raise their children well, sacrificing much to make certain their children would have a better future than they had had. I grew up, then, in a safe and sheltered environment. My family had enough food, enough work and the support of a huge community.

I was taught to treasure and respect hard work and to always honor and respect my family, my elders, and my country. I did so automatically and without question.

My family lived in Corte Madera, California, a small commuter town with excellent schools and a wonderful sense of community. I was an altar boy, a boy scout, an explorer scout and a good student. When I graduated from high school everyone expected me to go straight to the local junior college, and so, in the autumn of 1964, I did, intending to become an architect. But I was not prepared for college studies. I lacked the self-discipline and interest necessary to sustain the effort of studying. I was completely distracted by the freedoms of college life. I had a 1955 Chevrolet, a part-time job and a few dollars in my pocket. I enjoyed hanging out with my friends and living a life free of the overseeing eyes of high school teachers. Hence, after a single brief semester I found myself on academic probation.

In March of 1965 President Johnson ordered the bombing of Hanoi and the mining of Haiphong Harbor in Viet Nam. At the time, this was an action of which I was completely unaware. It became know as Operation Rolling Thunder'. Later that month the first U.S. combat troops, U.S. Marines, landed in Da Nang, Viet Nam, to protect the U.S. air base located there. Being too busy fooling around and enjoying my waning junior college life, I was unaware of these events. I had no idea I would be in Da Nang two years into the future.

At the end of my second semester I was dismissed from college. My failure came as a shock to my parents. I was the oldest of three sons and it was expected, as many parents of that era expected, that I would be more successful than they had been, and I would succeed by going to college. But I failed. I had high hopes and little understanding of how they might be fulfilled. I was intelligent, but I was young, confused and naive. I was sorry that I had disappointed my parents. I felt lost and uncertain about what my life was supposed to be and how I was to find it.

I began the summer of 1965 as an unemployed 18-year-old teenager. My parents had planned a cross-country trip to New York to visit my father's sister and her family and to attend the 1965 New York World's Fair. This adventure spared me the pressure from my parents to get a job. There was no point in accepting one were I to depart on vacation one month later.

My family and I began our eastern tour in July. We traveled by car, staying as we went in the Holiday Inns that had sprung up along the newly forming interstate highway system. It was a wonderful family trip, and it turned out to be the last time our whole family of five spent more than a few hours together. We traveled for nearly a month and spent two full weeks with my dad's sister's family in New City, New York. My memories of our travels are wonderful ones.

On our way home from New York we visited Washington, D.C. American military actions in Viet Nam had been building since late in the Kennedy administration, and as we walked through D.C., headlines in the local Washington newspapers announced that President Johnson had called for more troops in Viet Nam.[2] I was eighteen, my brother, David, was seventeen and our younger brother, Mark, was twelve. David and I read the headlines with trepidation. We knew that a draft was in effect. Just after we read the headlines we entered Arlington National Cemetery to view the gravesite of President Kennedy. As we passed from grave to grave and ultimately to the eternal flame at Kennedy's grave we were struck by sad emotions. I recall my brother David leaving in tears. I also knew that his tears, and the strange sadness I felt, were related more greatly to the headlines we had read than to the moving stillness of the proud soldiers interred around us. Our sadness was a premonition. We had led sheltered, pleasant lives and now it seemed things were about to change.

Immediately after our New York vacation I began looking for a job knowing that the draft loomed over me, a consequence of the loss of my college exemption. I thought there might be hope that I would not be called. I found

---

[2] This was, in fact, the initial call for the build-up of American troop strength in Viet Nam.

employment in San Francisco and began working as a file clerk in the design drafting department of Pacific Gas and Electric Company. I filed engineering and architectural drawings that were kept inside a walk-in, fireproof vault. The vault hosted an abundance of rubber bands that were used to contain drawings when they were rolled up for transport. My vault colleagues and I became experts in the art of shooting rubber bands at each other and anyone, other than the boss, who entered the vault. I performed this valuable service to mankind for eight full months.

In October I noticed and took a great interest in the beautiful young girl who had been living next door with her family for ten years. Her name was Lauren and she was fifteen years old. Our parents had purchased new homes adjacent to each other on the west side of Corte Madera in 1955. Lauren coming from a large Italian family, had two younger brothers and buckets of cousins, aunts, uncles, grand parents and family friends. Most of the kids on our block, including my two younger brothers and me, were boys. Lauren had two younger brothers and was one of the very few girls on our street.

Each and every major holiday Lauren's mother would bring Lauren over to our house to show her off to my mother, who had always wanted a girl. Lauren would be dressed to the nines in some darling outfit immaculately clean and carefully selected by her mother. My mother would say, "Harry, David and Mark, come out here and look at Lauren." This command would cause the three of us to march into our living room from wherever we were to scowl at Lauren. We'd make faces and feel uncomfortable as we stood while our mom praised Lauren and her cute outfit.

But when Lauren turned 15 my impression of her changed dramatically. She had blossomed into a beautiful girl.

Our first date was to a Friday-night football game. That year Lauren became my girlfriend (and years later my wife). Our football date took place in the autumn of 1965 as American troops continued to flow into South Viet Nam. I was vaguely aware of the increased action there and the build up of American troops, but only because I knew I might be called into the service by the draft board.

My draft notice arrived in the mail in January of 1966. I was ordered to report for a physical examination prior to induction into the service. I accepted this information with little emotion. My uncles, my dad and many others before me had received their draft notices in their time. This was simply my time.

In February I suffered the infamous embarrassments of a pre-induction military medical examination. A few weeks later I learned that I had passed my physical and I was ordered to report for induction into the service. On April 8, 1966, I went to the San Rafael bus depot and climbed onto a bus with forty or so other young men. I waived good-bye to my tearful parents and took a longing last look at Lauren. I felt a sense of loss and a sense of adventure. It was evident that life as I had known it was about to change dramatically. Deep inside I felt that my time to change from a boy to a man was near. It was a strange feeling of fear and anticipation. Twelve hours later I was fully immersed in boot camp at Fort Ord, California, and began the process of change.

During my first week at Fort Ord I was given a battery of examinations. Because I scored well on the exams, I was promptly offered an option. I could select my Military Occupational Specialty (MOS) in return for one year of additional military service[3]. The Viet Nam war had made its way to the nightly television news. Everyone viewed it as a strange war. It was presented as a war fought in jungles and hamlets. America's job was to pacify the country so that it could remain democratic and not communist. Special Forces, Green Berets, who were pictured as the super-modern pacifying warriors of the era, were undertaking this goal. There had been an increasing number of casualties reported on TV and in the press, but so far the American public was on board in support of the war. Regardless of its purpose and the visuals of American soldiers fighting and working for peace, I didn't want to be in the infantry. I was naïve but I was not ignorant of the role of an infantryman. My uncle had been one and had been captured by the German Army. I opted to become a radio relay and carrier repairman and to extend my time in the service to three years. I hoped I might wind up in Europe repairing electronic devices and thus avoid the increasingly dangerous conflict in Viet Nam. This was very wishful thinking.

Boot camp was everything Hollywood portrayed it to be. It was not only physically difficult, but it also required multitudes of "Yes sergeant" and "No sergeant" responses, thousands of push-ups, humiliating admonishments, inspections, weapons training, closed-course combat exercises, KP duty, guard duty, bayonet training, and team-building exercises. After nine weeks of boot camp I was physically fit and militarily compliant to obey orders. I was

---

[3] The normal active duty service requirement for a draftee was two years.

taught to understand that obedience and teamwork were keys to the overall safety of a military unit in combat. I also learned to smoke whenever there was a break, how to light a match and a cigarette in the wind, and how to curse with a very foul military mouth.

My fellow boot camp inductees were a cross-section of the middle and lower classes of the San Francisco Bay area. We were white, black and Hispanic; very few of us were Asian, we were the sons of clerks, bakers, mechanics, truck drivers, carpenters, fireman and policemen; hailing from places such as Berkley, Oakland, San Francisco, Hayward, Petaluma, Sonoma, and Richmond; a very few of us came from the more wealthy communities in Marin County. We came with long hair and beards, short hair and ties; in jeans, slacks, sport shirts, tee shirts, and no shirts; wearing shoes and sandals, and even barefoot. We were Protestants, Catholics, Jews, agnostics and atheists. Miraculously, after nine weeks we were formed into a disciplined group of uniformly fit, dressed, and obedient soldiers. All of our other attributes were hidden by the new façade of military behavior that had been indoctrinated into us.

I graduated from basic training in June and was sent home for two weeks of leave prior to continuing on in Signal School. My foul mouth embarrassed my mother and amused my dad, but they were glad to have me home and tolerated my minor foibles. They noticed a maturing change in me that they left unsaid, but that change and their pride showed in their eyes when I put on my uniform. I endeavored to spend most of my time with Lauren, but that was difficult. She was a sophomore in high school and both sets of our parents did their best to be proper chaperones.

In July I left home for Fort Gordon, Georgia, for training at the Army's Signal School. It was my first airplane flight. My family and Lauren saw me off at San Francisco International airport. I flew on a Boeing 707 from San Francisco to New Orleans and then on to Atlanta and August, Georgia. During our stop in New Orleans, the aircraft door was open to disembark and board passengers. As soon as it opened I broke into a heavy sweat. I didn't understand the phenomena. I had never been in a climate of extreme humidity. Little did I know that some months later I would spend a full year in one.

In signal school I learned how to operate and repair the radio and teletype communications systems used by the military within its theaters of operation. At that time a large portion of the Signal Corps was located in Europe supporting NATO and America's European activities in the Cold War, while a smaller part was located in Korea. I had hopes that I might be stationed in either Korea or Germany. I graduated from signal school in early January of 1967 and my thoughts of serving in Europe or Korea came to a halt. Most of my Signal Corps colleagues and I received orders for our disposition to Viet Nam. We were given a battery of vaccinations to ward off diphtheria, typhoid, yellow fever and a plethora of other illnesses. Then we were sent home on leave. Leave at this juncture was a cruel action.

I went home and brooded about my imminent departure to a war zone. My mother was devastated. She remembered her brother's departure into the army and his capture by the Germans in Italy during World War II. My dad was stoic, hiding his pride at having a son who would serve but simultaneously fearing for me. He had been in the Pacific during World War II. I was very much in love with my Lauren and wanted to avoid my departure to Viet Nam to prolong the wonder of being with her. It was an agonizing period of limbo, a time between the fantasies of youth and the impending realities of growth and it was compressed into a brief few weeks.

I was fearful, tearful and confused. I'd never been in a foreign country. My first solo adventure out of California had been to Fort Gordon, Georgia. Georgia had been a strange place as I experienced its hot, humid summer weather, slow pace and people with southern accents. Now I pondered about Viet Nam. Where the heck was it? What was there? There was a war there. Would I arrive with bullets flying and be in immediate danger? Would I be living deep in a green, Tarzan-like jungle? All these thoughts passed through my head along with thoughts of being away from my family.

I knew for certain that it was my job to serve my country and to be a brave and solid soldier[4]. My elders and their peers, those who had nurtured and raised me, had taught me this. They had served their country during World War II. While at home prior to going overseas, my dad and each of my uncles sought me out and in their own ways tried to impart the wisdom of their military and war experiences to me. Each one did so with love and concern. Nevertheless, each one failed miserably at communicating anything meaningful.

---

[4] In 1967 opposition to the war was growing and small protests were taking place, but the great swing toward massive and sometimes-violent protest had not yet occurred. It took the Tet Offensive of 1968 to turn the nation into bitter division. Most of us went to Viet Nam because we were taught that it was right to do our duty to our country. Most of us were under 20 years old and did not question our fate or our obligation.

These many years later I understand why they failed: It's impossible to express such experiences in a short time with a few brief words to someone who is young and has no experiences (no intellectually constructive connections) upon which to hang even a modicum of shared understanding.

At the end of my leave I said a tearful goodbye to Lauren and climbed into my parents' car for a trip across San Francisco Bay to the Oakland Army Terminal. I left behind my sad and concerned parents, my grandmother, assorted aunts, two younger brothers, a small army of proud but concerned uncles, and a battery of worried friends and neighbors. At the terminal I kissed my mother, shook hands with my dad, and walked through the gate and into the reception building.

CHAPTER 2 - INTO WAR

The Oakland Army Terminal was a very busy place of transition. It contained hundreds of troops on their way to Viet Nam. I received more vaccinations and then waited for several days in a state of limbo. Finally on the fourth evening, just after dark, a large group of us climbed on a bus and headed north to Travis Air Force Base. We traveled along the darkened freeway in silence, deep in our own thoughts. We arrived at the Travis terminal and were loaded onto a C-141 Starlifter, a four jet air transport fitted out to hold troops. The C-141 had a tail door that descended and turned into a ramp allowing small vehicles and supplies to be easily loaded aboard. When fitted out for troops, the aircraft had seats that faced backwards toward the tail of the aircraft. There were no amenities. The aircraft had no inner insulation or skin. It was cold and loud and we were given blankets and earplugs. As we took off into the late night we wondered where and how we would land.

Our first stop was Elmendorf Air Force Base in Alaska. It was 15 degrees and we were in short sleeved khakis. We ran full tilt from the plane to the terminal and waited for the aircraft to be refueled. On then to our next stop, the cold, snow-filled fields of Yokota Air Force Base in Japan; then on again to Viet Nam.

We flew for perhaps twenty or more hours through the night, across the International Date Line, through cold and snow on an aircraft without windows. As we approached Viet Nam we were disoriented and afraid. We began our descent feeling the loss of altitude and the change in speed and angle of the aircraft rather than seeing our downward progress through a window.   As we approached the runway at Ton Son Nhut Air Force Base near Saigon[5] the rear tail door of the aircraft began to lower.   It was almost fully deployed as we touched down and sped down the runway. Sitting backward and looking out the open door all we could see were the wiggling waves of heat rising from the runway. Our first impressions of Viet Nam were uniformly, "Oh my God it's a hot place." We strained to see outside. Was it safe?

As we disembarked from the aircraft, our eyes darted about in an effort to assess our new surroundings and our situation. Tan Son Nhut was a busy place.   There were aircraft and vehicles everywhere and there was a palatable bustle of urgency and purpose. We moved quickly as the non-commissioned officers responsible for our group herded us off the tarmac and onto several busses. The busses traveled rapidly away from the air base over a roughly paved road that passed through several small villages. The bus windows were covered with heavy external wire screens. We asked why and, to our shock, were told that the screens kept hand grenades from breaking through the glass windows and falling into the bus. I peered through the windows looking for other evidence of warfare. I saw only Army and Air Force equipment, vehicles and troops. I took in the foreign landscape and environment.

The villages we passed through were impoverished. Most buildings were loosely constructed of scavenged materials; only a few were built with brick or other masonry. Others were thrown together with a mixture of scrounged and recycled materials. Many had hand-painted signs advertising

---

[5] Saigon is now called Ho Chi Minh City.

14

ice, cigarettes and the inevitable Coca-Cola. The villages were interspersed in the very green and tropical Vietnamese countryside. The climate was hot and humid and the air carried a rotten smell that arose from the humidity and from the human feces that decayed in vacant lots. Outhouses, let alone modern plumbing, hadn't reached the countryside. The Vietnamese villagers eliminated their bodily waste in open fields.

I saw Vietnamese people walking about their villages and traveling on the road in tightly packed microbuses and on small motor scooters. They were uniformly slight people and they wore silk or linen clothing with a loose fit. They appeared to be a poor and benign people.

Our bus arrived at the 90th Replacement Battalion in Ben Hoa, a processing facility for new troops. The battalion was comprised of a huge tent city with a few solid buildings including a mess hall and some offices. I and the other new troops were kept busy clearing the tall grasses around the perimeter of the facility, building sand bag bunkers, and burning human waste from the battalion's out-houses. The waste was burned with gasoline in fuel barrel halves.

During our first night, we were introduced to the ever-present flares that hung in the sky to illuminate possible enemy positions. The flares were usually dropped from aircraft and fell to earth slowly as they hung from their small parachutes. As the flares loomed in the night sky, the few seasoned troops of the 90th Battalion told us tales of enemy infiltration, rocket attacks and skirmishes with the Viet Cong. These stories were half-truths intended to frighten us, but half-truths are exactly that. As our time in the country continued, we would discover the other halves. My sleep and my dreams that night were restless and uncomfortable.

After several days of waiting, I received orders to report to the 37th Signal Battalion in Da Nang. I knew only that this was somewhere North. I was transported by bus back to the Tan Son Nhut air base where I boarded a C-130 aircraft and began a trek north. The C-130 Hercules aircraft was a workhorse aircraft during the Viet Nam War. It had 4 turbo-prop engines, an overhead wing design, and a down-folding rear door that facilitated the loading of cargo and small vehicles. Like the C-141 Star Lifter that had brought me to Viet Nam, the C-130 had few windows and most troops traveling in it were unable to see the view outside the aircraft.

The first stop of my northern trek was Qui Nhon, a coastal town tucked between the sea and the coastal hills. Qui Nhon had a small air base and was a key stop along the American military's supply route that ran north and south along the Vietnamese coast. I got off the C-131 and waited at the Qui Nhon terminal for another plane to Da Nang. I struck up a conversation with another traveling soldier. He said, "You should have been here yesterday. There were rocks all over the place. They were coming in through the windows." I looked at him strangely wondering what he was talking about. I imagined the Viet Cong demonstrating outside and throwing rocks through the terminal windows. I finally discovered that he was speaking of R.O.K.s, Republic of Korea troops. The Korean government supported the American efforts in Viet Nam and had sent members of their Army into the country. Our guys called them ROKs. They had apparently passed en masse through Qui Nhon. My companion had a good laugh at my misunderstanding.

Travel in Viet Nam, even if you were in the Army, was not simple. Individual travel was on a space-available basis unless you were a V.I.P. All remaining flights to Da Nang that day were filled and I had to spend the night in Qui Nhon. I was sent to the 41st Signal Battalion where I was billeted for the night. The next morning I managed to find space on a flight to Da Nang on another C-130. I took off from Qui Nhon, once again bound for a foreign place while seated on a viewless aircraft.

I was completely surprised by the freedom I had to travel around Viet Nam. Not that I could go wherever I wanted. I had to take flights to my destination based on the orders that I carried. My surprise was that I traveled on my own and not with any particular unit. I was also surprised that the violence of war was so far not apparent. I had seen only illuminating flares. I had neither seen nor heard weapons fire, bombing or artillery fire. It was strange. If there was a war in this country, where was it?

I arrived in Da Nang after two full days of travel. Da Nang was in I Corps, the northernmost section of South Vietnam. It was the home of the one of the largest U.S. Air Force Bases in South Viet Nam. Like Tan Son Nhut, the Da Nang Air Base was bustling with activity. There were several other C-130 aircraft loading and unloading cargo and passengers, and I saw other larger transport aircraft not far away. In the distance I could see the tails of jet aircraft hidden in revetments along the runway. Then I heard the roar of jet aircraft as they took off. I went into the Da Nang terminal with four other servicemen. I found that they too were replacements headed for the 37th Signal Battalion. We reported to the front desk inside the terminal. The clerk on duty at the desk notified our battalion that we had arrived. In due time, soldiers from the 37th Signal arrived in a truck. They greeted us, and then we loaded our gear and climbed into the back of the truck headed for our new home. It turned out to be only a short quarter-mile drive away.

The air base had twin parallel runways. They were 10,000 feet long and ran from north to south. The 37th Signal Battalion was located just south of the mid-point and about four-tenths of a mile due east of the runways. While we traveled the short distance to our new Battalion we heard the constant roar of fighter jets taking off and landing along the runways of the air base. That sound would become a continuous background noise that we became completely accustomed to and eventually tuned out of our conscious hearing, until it stopped and we became aware of its absence.

Soon we drove through the gates of the 37th Signal Battalion compound. The Battalion had a tall water tower, two giant topographic and numerous other antennas. Barbed wire and guard towers surrounded it and the gate we had passed through was guarded by armed military police. It was evident that the 37th was a major signal installation. I was surprised to find that the battalion had barracks instead of tents. I learned that the French, who colonized Viet Nam, had built them when they operated in Viet Nam. The barracks and other buildings were white single story structures with slab floors, stucco walls, and corrugated steel roofs. The windows were made of screen and could be covered with shutters in the event of heavy rain or wind. The Battalion compound seemed well protected and safe and its barracks and buildings looked comfortable. The antennas and the large number of communications vans and equipment that were located about the facility gave it a very business-like and purposeful feeling. It seemed like a nice enough place.

CHAPTER 3 - INNOCENCE LOST

Upon our arrival at the 37th Signal Battalion, a staff sergeant took charge of us and billeted everyone but me in one of the barracks within the battalion's compound. Because the other new arrivals had filled the first barracks, I was separated from them, and billeted in a different barracks. Many of us had been through signal school at Fort Gordon. We had various signal skills: radio repair, radio operation, Teletype operator, cryptographer, cable lineman, and the like. Of course some of us were cooks, clerks, motor pool mechanics, and truck drivers. We also reflected the same overall demographic I had discovered in basic training; we were uniformly the sons of middle and lower class American families.

The next day, as new arrivals, we attended an orientation meeting during which we were briefed on the situation in Da Nang. We were told how to behave and what to expect. We were warned that the local water was bad and that we should drink only treated water or soda and beer. We were told that we should hire a mama-san[6] to do our laundry; that toilet articles and sundries could be purchased at the Base Exchange; that we would pull guard duty once a month; and that we would be assigned an M-14[7] rifle but it would be kept in the battalion armory until needed. We were informed that the local Vietnamese villagers were friendly and that Da Nang was a safe place. A young staff sergeant communicated all this information and more. He said that Da Nang had experienced only a few minor enemy skirmishes and that

---

[6] Mama-san was the American slang name for an older Vietnamese woman.
[7] Our unit had not been issued the newer M-16 rifle.

those had occurred around the perimeter of the marine-guarded airbase (of which we were inside). He concluded his portion of the orientation and turned the meeting over to a very crusty and much older sergeant major. The sergeant major (Top Kick) told us that he had been in the army since its brown-shoe[8] days when the army still used horses. He was blunt and used foul language. He said,

"Everything you just heard about being safe is pure bullshit. Just a few days ago they found some fucking gooks[9] outside the perimeter with a stash of mortars. There are sappers[10] all over this goddamn place. There's enemy walking all around here and we don't even know who the fuck they are. You keep your heads up at night and your asses down. That's all I've got to say."

The meeting adjourned. We left confused and a bit frightened. Who was right? The young staff sergeant or the crusty Top Kick? Why were there two views of the local situation?

The next day another new arrival and I walked to the Base Exchange to purchase shaving cream and other items. We were talking and found that we had both gone through Signal Corps training at Fort Gordon, Georgia. As we walked along we were approached by a group of Vietnamese children. They begged for candy, gum, cigarettes, and money and (in what turned out to be a classic pick pocket trick) they

---

[8] This was the early army when the boots that were issued were brown and had to be dyed black by the new servicemen.
[9] American troops called Vietnamese males "gooks". I don't know the origin of that term.
[10] Sappers are soldiers that infiltrate their enemies' perimeters to set explosive charges and destroy key positions and/or facilities.

began patting us. This was a new and confusing experience. We chased them away and continued on our walk. A few minutes later my new friend realized that his watch was gone. One of the children had snared it while the others were patting him. We were angry and disconcerted. The children seemed friendly, if poor. They were, in fact, crafty and hardened. It was a useful lesson.

A few nights later, I headed off to my barracks to sleep. I still hadn't been assigned a permanent bunk and the other new arrivals remained quartered in another barracks about one hundred feet away from mine. I had an upper bunk and I climbed up into it and fell into a deep restful sleep. I dreamed that I was back in physical education class at Redwood High School in Larkspur, California. Our class was dressed in our red gym shorts and grey tee shirts and we were in a group doing calisthenics. I was in the front rank. We stopped our exercises and stood at attention in our gym shorts. As we stood there a Fourth of July, cartoon style rocket flew parallel to us at eye level. It stopped in front of me and exploded. Ka-boom! With that ka-boom I awoke. I was disoriented and sleepy but I quickly gathered that we were under attack.

For most of us, this attack was our first time under fire. Even though we had endured boot camp, closed combat courses, and the like; we weren't prepared for the cruel reality of live ordinance launched at us by an enemy trying to kill us. As we woke to the unfamiliar sound of incoming rockets, our first reaction was to get up from our bunks and run. Unfortunately that reaction is deadly. Rockets and other ordinance explode up from their point of impact on the ground, into the air and outward. Standing up and running exposes a soldier to a greater possibility of injury from a blast's concussion and shrapnel. The best survival strategy is to get as close to the ground and as covered as possible. There was a Korean War veteran, a staff sergeant, in my barracks. He took immediate charge and hollered at us to lie on the floor next to the wall and cover our bodies with our mattresses. I remember doing exactly that and trying to press my face and body as far into the hard concrete floor as possible while praying "hail Mary full of grace". My heart was racing and my body trembled as the rockets fell toward us. Each rocket created a loud screeching sound that turned into a lower pitched chugging (almost like a train). As the rocket came overhead the chugging would stop and a pause of silence would follow before the rocket dropped and exploded in its full merciless fury. The pauses between the incoming chug of each rocket and their explosions seemed like eternities. Each pause gave us a brief moment to wonder where the rocket would hit. We heard some explode very close to us causing crunching and rattling sounds as they destroyed various structures and objects. We heard shrapnel whizzing through the air and hitting our building. We wondered if the next round would hit our barracks. While the rockets fell I prayed: "Hail Mary full of grace.....pray for us sinners now and at the hour of our death." Screech, chug, silence...."Hail Mary....." ...Ka-boom.

Half way into the attack the base's warning siren began a belated whine. We had heard and felt the rockets as they had fallen on our compound. Now their sound could be heard as they fell farther and farther away from our location and nearer to the Da Nang air base runway. When the rockets stopped falling we were told to get our weapons and take defensive positions along the perimeter of our installation.

We got up shaking and frightened, and ran to the armory where we grabbed any available rifle and as much ammunition as we could carry. A group of us ran to a ditch just inside our barb wired perimeter fence. We placed ourselves in prone positions and pointed our rifles through the barbed wire toward the road that ran alongside our compound. Several small fires had been started by the attack and flares had been launched into the night sky to illuminate the area. The fires and the flares painted an eerie glow over the surrounding road and the small buildings across the street. We didn't know what to expect. Would a ground attack follow? We looked guardedly at every shadow seeking out any form of movement. Fortunately nothing moved. An experienced sergeant told us to be calm and to keep the safeties on our weapons closed until ordered otherwise. Had we not received such a command, any one of us would have opened fire on the first moving object sighted. We were universally jumpy and alert.

As dawn broke, the shadows of the night slowly disappeared and we could begin to see all that was about us. The approaching daylight helped to diminish the terrors of the night and we calmed down and began to breathe normally. The night had brought terror and our enemy. The day seemed friendlier and was heartily welcomed.[11]

The all-clear command was finally given. We got up from our defensive positions, stowed our rifles and ammunition in the armory and began looking around. We counted heads and looked for our friends. We gawked at the damage as we

---

[11] Ever since that morning; daybreak has become for me a time of peace, a time of calm and a time of comfort. Over the months my buddies and I spent in Viet Nam we found that, in fact, the day *was* our friend and the night *was* our enemy.

walked about the compound. A considerable amount of equipment had been destroyed or damaged. Debris and shrapnel could be seen everywhere. One cryptographic trailer was in a shambles. A rocket had opened it like a tuna can. Another was partially damaged. Our Battalion commander was standing near it waving off film crews from one of the television networks. The trailer was wide-opened and contained classified communications devices that could not be filmed. The barracks where many of the new arrivals, except me, had been asleep had taken a direct hit through the roof. Many soldiers had been killed or wounded. Our compound had several new rocket craters scattered about its grounds. At least two fire trucks were still parked in the compound. Our commanders were walking about assessing the damage and trying to keep order.

I learned that my friend whose wrist watch had been stolen by the Vietnamese children a day or two earlier had been in the barracks that took the direct hit. He was killed in his sleep.[12] His barracks stood ominously. Its corrugated roof was ripped open and the supporting timbers were splintered and fallen into a heap. Debris filled the building's interior and it smelled of explosive residue. You could feel the death that had just invaded the structure. We walked past the building solemnly and with reverence.

Later that day our battalion commander, Lt. Col. Hollander, called us together to reassure us. He was a wonderful man with a strong sense of humanity that did not fit with the stereotypical military persona of most officers. He took the time to explain how to react during an attack. We were not

---

[12] Some 40 years later I visited the Viet Nam memorial wall in Washington, D.C. and found his name and the names of several others killed in the attack.

to get up and run (the natural reaction). He explained how our installation was not the main target of the V.C.; the air base was the target. He told us that we had been hit with 140 mm rockets. Until then, we were not certain what form of shell had fallen upon us. He listed our casualties, until then we were not certain how many of us had been killed and wounded.[13] The attack had occurred at 0315 hours (in the early morning) and lasted what seemed like an eternity but was probably less than 15 minutes. Fifty-six rockets had been launched. Thirteen had fallen within our small compound. Within the Da Nang perimeter eleven soldiers had been killed. Eight of them had died with the direct hit on our barracks. Fifteen 37th Signal Battalion soldiers had been wounded. A total of 124 military personnel around the air base had been wounded. The Viet Cong had been aiming for the aircraft positioned in revetments next to the Da Nang runway. The 37th Signal Battalion lay between the launch site of the rockets and the air base's aircraft revetments. As the Viet Cong walked the Rocket fire toward the runway, their first dozen or so rockets fell short of their intended mark hitting the 37th Signal. It was likely that our installation's prominent topographic antennas and our water tower served the Viet Cong well as sighting monuments. One of our sensitive and classified cryptographic trailers was hit and completely destroyed. Lt. Col. Hollander commended us for our efforts and explained that we would be better prepared for the next attack. What he did not tell us, what we did not yet understand but would realize over the next

---

[13] February 27, 1967: NVA rocket troops launched 140 mm rockets against the Da Nang Air Base. More than 50 rockets hit the base in less than a minute. The rockets had a range of 6 miles. This was the first known use of large tactical rockets in South Viet Nam. The use of these weapons forced marines guarding Da Nang to extend their protective perimeter out to 6 miles. This added great strain to the marine's manpower.

months, was that we had been initiated into the irreversible status of hardened soldiers. The rockets of combat had violated us. We had begun the process that erodes then ends innocence, toughens the mind, and murders the high hopes of youth.

CHAPTER 4 - DA NANG 1967

Da Nang was the major base for operations in Northern South Viet Nam (I Corps). However, in 1967 my unit, the 37th Signal Battalion, was one of a very few U.S. Army groups in Da Nang. The Air Force had the largest number of personnel followed by the Marines and the Navy. Later in 1967 many more army personnel passed through Da Nang as the army began strengthening I Corps. I Corps' ground operations had been left largely to the U.S. Marines until then.

The Da Nang air base was the prominent installation in the area. Air Force, Marine and civilian aircraft flew in and out of Da Nang air base twenty-four hours a day. At one time it was the busiest airport in the world. The most obvious aircraft were F-4C Phantom fighters. They were twin-engine jets that took off in tandem with their afterburners blazing and their engines deafening all ears. Even their landings were unique as they utilized small parachutes to slow their ground speed.

The Navy operated the military port of Da Nang and provided I Corps with equipment and supplies. The Navy also operated Swift Boats that patrolled the waters and rivers in and around Da Nang. And, of course, my small U.S. Army installation operated military communications systems for Da Nang.

All of Da Nang's military personnel and assets had to be guarded and made safe from the enemy.

And as is usually the case, this job fell to The U.S. Marines. They guarded both the Da Nang Air Base and the port. Their perimeter extended about three miles from the center of Da Nang to the surrounding countryside to the north, east and south. The South China Sea bordered the West. During my time in Da Nang, the Viet Cong's use of 122 mm and 140 mm[14] rockets required that the Marine perimeter be extended to approximately six miles, the effective limits of the rocket's range. The Marines had a tough job. While the rest of us worked in reasonably safe and comfortable conditions, they were disbursed in the rice paddies and fields around Da Nang and frequently in nighttime combat. I have enormous respect for the U.S. Marine Corps. The Marines had a squadron of F-8 Crusader aircraft that flew in support of their ground troops. The Crusaders operated from the Da Nang Air Base and also from their base located to the south in Chu Lai.

With the exception of the Marines, all of the military personnel in Da Nang lived and operated within the confines of the Da Nang perimeter in old or newly pre-fabricated buildings or tents set up on wooden platforms. Every major unit operated a small city of personnel containing the unit's living quarters (buildings or tents), toilet facilities, mess halls, and headquarters facilities. Most everyone slept in bunks or on cots (with a mattress) and enjoyed about 32 square feet of space (including a locker and/or foot locker for clothing and personnel belongings). Those who lived in tents often called their tents hootches, a name also used for many of the ramshackle homes Vietnamese families assembled from scrap materials.

---

[14] This is the diameter of the shell. 120 mm is approximately 4 ¾ inches. 140 mm is approximately 5 ½ inches.

My fellow soldiers and I lived in old single story French built barracks. They had slab floors and cinder block walls covered with white stucco. Each barracks contained bunk beds, metal lockers and footlockers. The barracks slept about thirty personnel. Our toilets and showers were contained in a separate building shared by three or four other barracks. We had one large mess hall built in the same style as our French-built barracks.

I was a Radio Relay and Carrier Repairman[15]. I diagnosed and repaired microwave radios, frequency modulators, and radio Teletype equipment. All of this equipment was made to fit compactly into a communications van that, in turn, fit into the back of a deuce and a half[16] or could be strapped up and lifted by a helicopter for transport. Each van of equipment employed a separate electrical generator and a 30-foot antenna. These portable communications stations[17] operated up and down the coast of Viet Nam, located approximately twenty-five miles apart. They communicated with each other via microwave radios whose antennas were arranged in a line-of-sight path with each other. Each communications station received a microwave signal from another station and then boosted and relayed that signal to the next station. The microwave signals carried multiple frequencies of signals, each frequency carrying either voice or Teletype signals. The signals were disassembled at their destination into individual messages. Many of the messages were encrypted and were secret or top secret in nature. This system and others (including Topographic Radio Signaling and traditional telephone systems) provided the military

---

[15] My military occupational specialty (M.O.S.) was 31L20.
[16] A two and a half ton truck
[17] They were designated AN/MRC-69 Radio Relay Systems.

forces in Viet Nam with the vital communications needed to conduct their military operations. The relay systems whose equipment I repaired were located within I Corps[18]. They ran down the coast from near the DMZ in Dong Ha to Quang Tri, Hue, Phu Bai, Da Nang, Chu Lai, Hoi An, Tam Ky and other locations all the way to Qui Nhon.

The 37th Signal Battalion was the primary hub for communications in Da Nang. My battalion provided phone services much like a local hometown telephone company. Its crews operated a telephone system consisting of overhead telephone cables and telephones that were distributed in and around the military installations of Da Nang. We also operated and maintained the various radio communications systems that connected U.S. forces in Da Nang with our military forces in the rest of the country. The 37th's compound was approximately three acres in size. It was surrounded by barbed wire fencing, defensively positioned bunkers, and five guard towers. Two topographic antennas sloped up 35 to 45 feet high in the center of the facility and were a substantial landmark, especially for rockets. A 40-foot water tower and numerous other antennas increased the Battalion's prominence and underlined its proximity to the Da Nang Air Base runways. The installation was filled with several semi-truck-sized cryptographic trailers, buildings containing communications equipment, radio relay equipment vans, warehouses for equipment storage, various trucks and repair vehicles, electrical generators, a maintenance facility (where I worked), barracks, a mess hall, and two headquarters buildings. A single main gate, guarded

---

[18] South Viet Nam was divided up by the military into four sections or corps: I Corp (called "eye" corps) extending from the DMZ to just north of Quang Tri, then from north to south in succession; II Corps, III Corp, and IV Corp.

by military police opened to the main road of the Da Nang Air Base.

CHAPTER 5 - A SECOND ATTACK

I served my fair share of guard duty during the first two thirds of my Viet Nam tour. After I gained the rank of Specialist 5, that form of duty ended. The 37th Signal Battalion in Da Nang had five guard towers intermixed with the barbed wire fencing around its perimeter. They were constructed of heavy wooden timbers, had wooden floors and walls and corrugated metal roofs. The inside walls were lined with sand bags to provide the guard on duty with some protection from small arms fire. Each tower had one or two floodlights that illuminated the area directly in front of the tower just outside the fence of the compound. Each tower had a field telephone that connected to the compound's headquarters building and the officer of the day. A single ladder located inside the compound accessed the towers. I spend at least a dozen nights on guard duty in these towers.

The vicinity of the Da Nang Air Base was flat and the view from the various guard towers was excellent. Aircraft could be seen taking off and landing along the air base runways, and lights from the surrounding military installations and local villages dotted the darkened landscape. The Da Nang area was on constant alert for nighttime incursions by the enemy. In addition, the Marines patrolled the perimeter areas of Da Nang. The perimeter began about six miles from the center of the air base extending north, east and south of that location. When enemy nighttime action was suspected or observed, the local patrols would launch flares to illuminate the area of suspected action. The flares hung from small parachutes and lit both the ground below and the surrounding night sky. There were often 3 or 4 flares operating at any given hour of the night. Most of the time, they were located outside the six-mile perimeter. When we saw flares nearer to our compound, we worried.

An aircraft nicknamed "Puff the Magic Dragon" or simply "Puff" was often used to suppress suspected or real enemy activity. Puff operated with a call sign of "Spooky" and was sometimes also referred to by that name. "Puff" was the singular name of what were actually several AC-47 (the civilian nomenclature is the more familiar DC-3) fixed wing aircraft that employed Gatling guns. Three Gatling guns were positioned in the open side door of each aircraft. The guns fired bullets at the rate of 6,000 rounds per minute. Every fourth round was a tracer. Puff would drop one or two 200,000 candle power flares over a target area and then fly in a circle around the area of ground they illuminated. It could then fire its Gatling guns at the ground below and spray the land with hundreds of bullets, annihilating anyone or anything located there. When it operated, it looked like it was hosing the ground with a stream of fire, hence it garnered its name, "Puff the Magic Dragon", a flying dragon that appeared to breathe fire. Puff was a beautiful but deadly nighttime sight as it fired its guns and flew around its flares. I had my Minolta single lens reflex camera and I often set it on a long exposure to photograph Puff. I tried this several times, usually taking my pictures from the guard towers. I didn't have a telephoto lens and most of my pictures show only a miniature view of Puff far off in the distance. I often wished that Puff would operate nearer to our compound so that I could obtain a better photograph of it. This wish came true in early January and as the saying goes, "Be careful what you wish for."

While on guard duty, one could observe the many night-time sights and activities of the Da Nang war zone: the multiple flares, the fires of the distantly operating Puff, the lights and afterburner flames of F4 Phantom aircraft taking off, the lights of helicopters operating in the distance, village and base lights, and the lights of jeeps and other vehicles making their way through the streets of the area. If one were on guard duty on the right night at the right time one might even witness a rocket attack. I found myself in that very situation on the night of March 15, 1967.

The normal activities and sights were evident from my view from the guard tower. The tower faced south and looked directly toward the end of the air base runway just under a mile away. A rocket attack began somewhere between midnight and 0400 hours. I first heard the weak puffing swoosh of the first rocket as it was launched. I glanced in the direction of the noise and saw a faint flicker of light and a slight but evident stream of faint light trailing the path of the rocket. I watched somewhat spell bound never having seen a rocket in flight[19]. My brain didn't register what I saw as threatening until the rocket hit the end of the air base runway and exploded, showering its impact area with a spray of white-hot shrapnel. The explosion was surprisingly beautiful. Then another rocket hit the air base and my brain immediately switched from its foreign state of objective observation to survival mode. Suddenly I was on the ground beneath the guard tower behind a sandbag with my rifle loaded and pointed outside the compound. I have no memory of climbing down the tower ladder. I don't recall jumping from the tower. One second I was standing in it watching an attack, the next I was in a defensive position some sixteen feet below. My brain examined the dangers of

---

[19] I couldn't actually see the rocket, only the semi-lit arc of its path through the air.

a sixteen foot high exposure to a possible attack, the minimal protection of a wooden tower and a few sand bags, the possibility of a tower collapse caused by a nearby explosion, and the high profile of a single soldier standing behind a shining light. It crunched the numbers in record time, examined the physical condition of the body it operated, the height of the tower, the number of steps in the tower's ladder, the length of time necessary to move said body along the ladder, the frequency and proximity of the incoming rockets, the softness and condition of the ground below the tower, and the extent of any injuries that might be suffered from a sixteen-foot jump. It recognized the fear exhibited by its owner, analyzed all of its owner's vital functions and executed a marvelous escape from the tower. I am fairly certain that I jumped. I was on the ground in an area of sand that had been spilled from the sand bags around the tower. I suppose that the sand softened the impact of my jump, but I really have no idea at all how I got out of the tower.

This was the second rocket attack in Da Nang[20]. It proved that the first one, in February, had not been a fluke. Our commanders began to take the likelihood of more rocket attacks very seriously. On March 16th, the day after the second attack we began to fortify our battalion compound. I spent the entire day filling sandbags and building bunkers. Recoilless rifle and machine guns sites were added to the compound's defenses. Each of us began to question our safety in Da Nang.

---

[20] The enemy attacked the Da Nang Air Base with over 10 rounds of 140mm Russian spin-stabilized rockets. Sixteen US soldiers were wounded. Aircraft and runway damage was negligible. Reaction forces located 23 launchers and 11 rockets on the east bank of the Yen River, 11km southwest of the base. (From the web site: armchairgeneral.com)

CHAPTER 6 - THE RICE PADDY INN

I was fortunate that I was not in Vietnam in the infantry or otherwise outside a secure base. My job was the repairing of radio equipment and I worked hard and diligently doing that work on the swing shift from 6 p.m. to 2 or 3 p.m. Monday through Friday. I slept from 4 or 5 in the morning until 11 or 12. That left 6 hours each day and all day on the weekends with nothing much to do. So I looked to fill my time with some suitable activity.

The 37th Signal Battalion compound had an N.C.O. club called the Rice Paddy Inn. A small group of higher-ranking NCO's oversaw the facility. The Inn had a full bar, a small stage, a sound system and a few dozen tables with chairs. It sold beer, wine, and hard liquor by the drink for twenty-five cents each. Anyone from private to general could enjoy this club however; officers did not generally show up as they had their own club in downtown Da Nang.

I was paid $275 a month. I sent $200 home to my family to be saved and $40 to my girl friend, Lauren, for her high school tuition. That left me with $25. For $2.50 I could purchase a book of ten chits, or stamps, each of which could be redeemed for an alcoholic beverage at the Rice Paddy Inn. My other expenses were for laundry and toilet articles and did not amount to very much money. So I drank quite a bit.

Early in my tour while drinking at the Rice Paddy Inn, I found that the place was in need of a bartender, specifically someone that could work from 2 in the afternoon until 5 in the evening, and nights on weekends. I fit the bill and was hired.

My routine became one of sleeping from 4 am until noon, having personal time from noon until 2 pm, working as a bartender from 2 pm until 5, and working my electronic maintenance shift from 6 pm until 2 am. I had Saturday and Sunday mornings off and worked at the bar those days from 6 pm until after midnight. I was paid $1.25 an hour for my labor and sent some of that money home.

As a bartender I met all sorts of folks. The Rice Paddy Inn was open to all military and authorized civilian personnel in Da Nang. One needed only to pass through the security at the guarded gate of the 37th Signal Battalion in order to gain entry to the Inn. So I met Air Force, Marine and Naval personnel as well as civilian contractors. All came to the Rice Paddy Inn to relax and drink. Many brought stories about their time in the country and rumors of what they expected would happen next. As I talked with them I began to learn about the breadth of the war and its confusing purpose and unconventional conflicts.

The Inn had live entertainment most Saturday nights. There was a regular entertainment circuit that operated along the Western Pacific Coast of Asia. Musical bands, dancers and other acts performed at various military clubs up and down the coast of Viet Nam and in Thailand, the Philippines and Japan. Most of the performers were Asian. Their music was largely rock and roll and very entertaining.

I was amazed to discover that there also existed an entire industry of bar and liquor supplies. A salesman visited the Rice Paddy Inn regularly to meet with the NCO manager of the club. Orders for glasses, napkins, liquor and other bar supplies were then placed with this salesman. The liquor was high quality. It included Johnny Walker Scotch, Crown

Royal, Jack Daniels Kentucky Sour Mash, and other high-end brands. Most of the beer, unfortunately, was of lesser quality and included the Philippine San Miguel.

Drugs were not an apparent issue during my 1967 tour in Viet Nam. They became a serious problem some years later after my departure from the country. Drugs were around, however. One Vietnamese man who worked as a parts clerk in the electronic maintenance lab smoked opium three times a day but no one bothered him or seemed to care. Alcohol, however, was a problem. I drank and got drunk many times, and some of my friends got absolutely blitzed frequently. We did not drink while on duty. On the other hand, it was not a good thing when one found oneself drunk during a rocket attack.

On special days, such as New Years Eve, the Fourth of July, and St. Patrick's Day, the Rice Paddy Inn would be decorated for the occasion and usually had special entertainment. The place would be packed to the gills with soldiers and civilians and the alcohol would flow like water into the thirsty mouths of all. New Years Eve was especially raucous. The club hired a band and a stripper. When I returned to our barracks after midnight, I found one of my friends naked on the floor and nearly unconscious from alcohol. Thank God I never got that drunk.

The Rice Paddy Inn served as the major social release for multitudes of armed forces personnel. Not surprisingly, it operated at a profit. All proceeds were reinvested into the facility. My job there boosted my small income and allowed me to save money for my return to the United States.

CHAPTER 7 - THE U.S.0.

Two days after our second rocket attack the U.S.O brought the country musician Roy Acuff to Da Nang. He and his band set up on a flat bed trailer not far from the Da Nang Air Force Base and a short walk from my Army compound. My friends and I enjoyed an hour-long performance complete with Roy's amazing fiddling. It was a surreal experience. Here was very American country music preformed by boot-wearing, hat-flying, fiddling musicians juxtaposed against the backdrop of a fully operating base of warfare, with the noise of military aircraft accenting the music. I wish I could have recorded the event.

The U.S.O. provided the armed forces in Viet Nam with much appreciated services. They operated the hamburger stand at China Beach and they provided art materials, books and other items of diversion. And, once in a while they brought big name entertainers like Roy Acuff into the country.

Most Americans remember Bob Hope's many treks overseas to entertain the armed forces. His road trips were a the highlight of the U.S.O.'s entertainment efforts. He came to the Da Nang area just before Christmas in 1967, but getting a seat to see him was difficult and not all soldiers were able to get off duty or out of the field to see him. I was one who missed his show. I do remember the extremely heightened level of security at Da Nang on the day he performed.

I did manage to get to a performance of *Hello Dolly* held at the same outdoor theater used by Bob Hope. The performance starred the wonderfully talented and funny Martha Raye. She was marvelous and her show was most entertaining. Ironically, it would have been unlikely that I would have gone to a musical comedy as a civilian back in the states. In fact, the next live theater performance I attended was *Hair* in 1969. But there I was thoroughly enjoying *Hello Dolly* in Da Nang, Viet Nam.

In April my electronic maintenance officer selected me and some other soldiers to go on a U.S.O.-sponsored boat trip. Really?

On a fine Saturday morning we left the perimeter of the air base and rode through downtown Da Nang. It was the first time I had been in Da Nang City. It was beautiful. The French influence was abundant in the architecture, and large tropical trees shaded the main streets. We rode along the waterfront on a street with the water on one side and homes and shops on the other. Then we reached a marina filled with fishing boats. We climbed aboard one of the fishing boats and set out into the main channel. We had our rifles, ammunition, a radio, beer, soda, and sandwiches. We were going on a wartime picnic of sorts.

Our 30-foot boat motored along the Da Nang City waterfront and then set a course along the north side of Monkey Mountain. We stayed close to the shore and kept watch for any activity along the coastal side of the rising Monkey Mountain hills. There was none.

After forty-five minutes or so our boat put in to a small cove at the base of the mountain. We anchored and stripped down to our shorts. Then with one person on watch on-board, we leapt into the water and enjoyed a fine swim. The

U.S.O. even provided snorkeling equipment. One of my friends dove deep into the sea and came up with a Vietnamese lobster. After laughing at the idea of such a creature, we threw it back into the sea and swam to the small beach at the end of the cove. There we lazed away the day drinking beer, eating our sandwiches and swimming. It was a lovely day. While we partied on the beach, our rifles and ammunition remained on the boat. I wondered later what we would have done had we come under attack. Late in the afternoon we reversed our travels and went back to Da Nang. That evening I was back in my quarters amazed at the picnic I had attended in the middle of a war zone.

God bless the U.S.O.

CHAPTER 8 - RUMORS AND ALERTS

In a war zone filled with secrecy, rumormongering becomes acute. My unit found itself especially susceptible to the spinning of rumors because most of the secret communications necessary for war operations flowed through its Signal Corp equipment. Almost 100 percent of the rumors predicted when we would next be "hit" with enemy rockets or sapper attacks. These rumors stemmed from the "military intelligence" messages allegedly overheard or seen by the unit's communications equipment operators. Rarely a week went by without someone intimating that sergeant Jones said, "I saw a message that indicates the V.C. are planning an attack tomorrow night." or private Smith who works in the cryptographic van says "don't go to sleep tonight until after 0400 hours". Very few of these warnings proved accurate[21], yet because of the real threat and experiences of attack and the plausibility of the rumors' sources, everyone listened attentively and reacted fearfully to what they heard.

On March 18th our commander assembled us and told us that intelligence had received information that we were to be attacked that night. We spend the afternoon adding sandbags to our bunkers, lighting the walkways between our barracks and the armory, and dispersing all of the battalion's vehicles. A first aid team was formed, extra guards were posted, and spotters were put in position. That night we took our mattresses off our bunks and put them on the floor. We spent the night on the floor next to the barracks

---

[21] The one rumor or warning that stands out as auspicious and that set the stage for all the others was the one offered by the unit's first sergeant during our orientation (see Chapter 3).

walls. Nothing at all happened. About 0300 hours an all clear was issued. The intelligence had been wrong and we were universally relieved that that was the case.

Five days later, in the early morning hours of March 23 a boom and the base siren awakened us. We took cover expecting the sound of incoming rockets, but the noises we heard were different. We heard huge explosions coming from the direction of the southern end of the air base runway. When we arrived in our defensive positions we could see large balls of flame and smoke rising from the end of the runway. An F-6 fighter had collided with a C-141. The pilots of the F-6 had managed to eject, but the entire crew of the C-141 had been killed. The C-141 was carrying 500-pound bombs and napalm. The bombs and napalm exploded and burned white hot. The next morning all that remained of the C-141 was its tail section. It sat at the end of the runway as a grim memorial of the night's tragedy.

The month of March set a pattern for the rest of our tour in Da Nang. There were many more nights of rumored attack, actual attack, and other disruptive, frightening events. All of us became attuned to the noises of the night and especially sensitive to the sounds of explosions. These sensitivities never left us.[22] About this time in my tour I wrote my girlfriend, Lauren, a letter telling her that we were all OK but that most nights we were nervous wrecks.

---

[22] Ten years after my return from Viet Nam a garbage truck dropped a refuse container to the ground six feet behind me while I walked along Montgomery Street in San Francisco. It produced a very loud bang that sent me flying to the pavement next to the wall of the adjacent building. Years later I was continually shaken by the loud sound of very unstable classroom desks that occasionally fell over while my back was turned to my class while I wrote on the classroom's white boards.

Work to repair the barracks damaged by the February rocket attach began a few days after that attack. The roof was rebuilt and replaced, all of the damaged metal lockers and bunks were removed, the screen windows were repaired, and the inside walls and floor were patched and painted. All of us who worked in the maintenance lab were moved into the newly repaired barracks, even some of the guys that had been in it during the attack. It was a nice clean barracks, but it still carried the onus of having been the one that had taken the hit and the one in which seven soldiers had died.

One of our guys was a black fellow from the Deep South named Moton. He was a short young man with a heavy southern drawl. Like the rest of us, he had been through the February rocket attack and the attack of March 15th. Now, all of us were living in the repaired barracks. We were in our bunks about 0400 hours one morning when the base siren sounded. All of us except Moton reacted in unison by jumping out of our bunks, covering ourselves with our mattresses, and compressing ourselves between the concrete floor and walls. Moton sat up in his bunk and screamed. His was not an ordinary scream. It was a blood-curdling, banshee like scream of sheer terror. Moton screamed for what seemed like five minutes before someone grabbed him and threw him to the floor and cover. Eventually the base siren ceased and an all clear was issued. No rockets had fallen and whatever had prompted the siren's sounding had been dealt with. We climbed up from the floor. Later in the morning our sergeant went to Moton and talked with him. He explained that Moton's scream was worse than the threat of attack, that it terrified us more than the rockets, and that it was dangerous to simply scream; a soldier had to take immediate cover. Then, with considerable understanding, compassion, and a sense of humor; our sergeant gave Moton a whistle. He told Moton, "If we are ever under the threat of attack again and you have the urge to scream, please take cover first and then blow this whistle." We experienced more rocket attacks and more false alarms and Moton didn't scream. He didn't blow the whistle either.

CHAPTER 9 - CONTRADICTIONS

Viet Nam was full of surprises and contradictions. One day we would be at the beach or the movie theater, and then a few days later rockets would rush in killing, maiming and terrifying us.

China Beach[23] was but a few short miles from our compound. It was, and still is, a lovely stretch of wide, white sandy beach on the South China Sea west of Da Nang. The beach sits along a rounded bay formed by Da Nang's shores and the peninsula containing Monkey Mountain to the North. It's a picturesque and beautiful location. China Beach was a Marine rest and recuperation (R & R) center; Marines were sent there for two or three days to get away from the war and to rest and recuperate from their combat duties. It also hosted a USO facility that offered hamburgers, hot dogs, volleyball and beach equipment. You could go to the beach for the day and pretend you were at a beach at home. However, there were exceptions to the homelike atmosphere. First, there were no women or children at the beach. It was populated nearly 100 percent by young American military men. Because of the war, no one in his or her right mind would hang out at the beach after dusk. There were snakes in the ocean. Yes, snakes. A group of us were casually swimming in the surf when several large snakes

---

[23] There was a television show called "China Beach" that aired several years ago. In that show, a beautiful young military nurse dealt with the horrors and realities of the Viet Nam War as she performed her duties at an Army hospital allegedly located at China Beach. I chuckle when I think of that television show. I recall no women at all, let alone beautiful women. I remember the USO facilities as stark and unglamorous, and I have no idea whether or not there was a hospital at China Beach

were spotted nearby swimming just outside the surf line. We evacuated the water quickly. Finally, there were no hotels or air-conditioned bars along the beach and there was very little shade. Our treks to the beach usually consisted of a quick dip in the ocean, a brief stay on the beach, and a hamburger and a beer at the USO. Beach trips were a refreshing break from the daily grind of our military lives.

One afternoon we were warned by our battalion commander that "intelligence" had reported a high likelihood of attack. We spent the night sleeping on the floor on our mattresses near the concrete walls. Extra guards were once again posted and the first aid team was again awake for the night on full alert. Once again the "intelligence" proved to be wrong. Although we were grateful that an attack hadn't occurred, we found ourselves, once again, stressed and exhausted. We existed night after night in a state of hyper alertness and it was wearing us down. Despite our mental fatigue it was better to be sensitized, alert, and sleepless than to be exposed for an extra instant or two while enemy rockets rained in on you.

Early in the morning on May 6th a very loud boom chased us from our beds to the floor. The base siren whined immediately after the boom and we kept our prone positions on the floor waiting for another explosion or boom. None followed. The all clear was issued within several minutes of the initial boom and siren. We scratched our heads and tried to catch a few more minutes of rest before dawn broke. Later in the morning we learned that a friendly artillery battery had fired a short round. The round fell far "short" of its distant target landing near the air base. No one was hurt, but the dangers of the night had once again validated our constant state of mental and bodily alertness.

Later in the month of May, during the day when our nerves were resting from the tension of the night, my company held a barbeque. My friend Zeke had traded liquor for a case of New York steaks. Others found a barbeque grill and someone went into Da Nang and purchased dozens of freshly baked French rolls. We, of course, had plenty of beer and soda. Most of us cut our bread open to make steak sandwiches. To our surprise the rolls were dotted inside with tiny black specks. At first I thought the specks were poppy seeds that had been added to the bread for flavor, and then the others and I realized that the specks were really small gnats. Each small loaf of French bread was filled with hundreds of gnats. They'd landed on the bread dough while it rose and were kneaded into the bread before it was baked. No one had had French bread for months and the gnats were small, so we bit into the rolls and ate them despite their extra ingredients.

The month of May passed slowly followed by other months of routine daytime work, occasional recreational activities, and long stressful nighttime alerts, false alarms and actual attacks. We lived in a completely dysfunctional world of contrasts - contrasts between day and night and rest and terror.

CHAPTER 10 - THE FOURTH AND FIFTEENTH OF JULY

The day of July 4, 1967 was just another routine wartime day. Not much happened. However, the night of the 4th was wild. Sometime after dark the urge to celebrate overcame all form of discipline. An abnormal number of flares were launched, troops fired their weapons, and artillery batteries fired their most brilliant ordinance. The night sky was filled with live ammunition and loaded with the streaming fire of tracer rounds. It was an impressive demonstration of American military firepower. It was beautiful and damn scary. It was also dangerous, because what goes up must come down somewhere. It's amazing no one was killed or wounded by all the stray rounds. The display lasted for nearly half an hour before the base commanders managed to garner some control. Although it was a wonderful and colorful celebration, it was uncontrolled and frightening. It turns out it was an ominous display of the real fire power that would come two weeks later.

I was working in the Electronic Maintenance lab on the night of July 15, 1967. My shift was due to end at 0200. Twenty minutes past midnight the first of many rockets screamed toward the Da Nang runway and exploded. I dove to the floor while the fluorescent lights in the lab's ceiling fell from their sockets and shattered on the floor. The base siren wailed. I ran to the armory for my M-14 and then headed for the bunker outside the maintenance facility. Rockets were raining less than a mile to the south. I could see them exploding through the gun port of my bunker. The bunker was dug into the ground and it was covered with sandbags. The gun port opened with a view about a foot above ground level, facing south and east across the southern end of the runway. I watched as more rockets fell at the end of the runway. Eventually one or more rockets hit the air base ammunition dump. I estimate that I was about a half a mile from the resulting explosion. The ammo dump erupted with an apocalyptic blast. It offered me a lesson in physics I will never, ever forget. The shocks from the blast traveled at differing times through the air and the earth. First the night sky became instantly bright like the sun. The brightness was presented as a flash that dimmed very slowly from blinding to soft orange. It was followed by a blast of heat that shocked me as it warmed my face. The heat shock was followed by the booming sound of the blast, which was followed, in turn, by a ground wave that lifted me up and plopped me back down. After these four successive shocks (light, heat, sound and quake), fire and smoke from the explosion billowed and ascended upward into the night sky. Ten to thirty seconds after the blast, debris and shrapnel descended from the sky and fell about the bunker. The debris continued to fall for many minutes after the blast. A small city of newly constructed and occupied Air Force barracks was located in the vicinity of the blast. As I sat in my bunker I prayed for the airmen living there who must have been very near to ground zero.

The attack lasted ten or 15 minutes but the resulting fires and explosions continued throughout the night and into the next morning. The air base suffered considerable damage. Eight Americans were killed and 175 were wounded.[24] Our

---

[24] July 15, 1967: Stand-Off Rocket Attack begins (at Da Nang Air Base) at 0020 hours. At 0040 hours, the second volley of rounds hit a stack of 250 lb. bombs in the ammo dump that went off like the Fourth of July. Bomb fragments were everywhere. A brilliant flash turned night to day as if a nuke had exploded. A shock wave swept the base with heat and blast as the bomb dump exploded

compound was untouched but our nerves were shattered. We had suffered damage and death in late February and there had been several attacks and alerts since then. This attack was significant because of its size, duration, and damaging results. Clearly the problem of rocket attacks was becoming worse rather than better and the progress of the war as observed from Da Nang did not seem to fit the progress reported in the Stars and Stripes[25].

On Sunday morning, July 16, 1967, the morning following the rocket attack, I went to mass along with five or six other guys from my battalion. The Catholic mass was packed to overflowing. The small base chapel was bursting at the seams with airmen, seaman, marines, civilians and soldiers. The major attack of the prior night reminded all of us of our mortality, so we flocked to the familiar and comforting reassurances of the mass. A young Catholic Air Force chaplain said mass. After the gospel reading he began his homily. He explained that he had only been in the country for a few weeks and that he was as afraid and terrified by the events of the past night as we were. He had spent the early morning after the attack making rounds in the air base hospital. The hospital was situated very near an air force

---

hurtling fire and debris thousands of feet into the air. Shrapnel rained for several minutes. Eighty three (83) Rounds of 122mm Rockets, 140mm Rockets, and mortars were received. Damage and carnage: USA; 10 Aircraft Destroyed, 49 Aircraft Damaged, 8 KIA, 175 WIA. Da Nang's twin runways and taxiways were closed for 12 hours. The Stand-Off Rocket attack of July 15, 1967 was the deadliest attack of the war at Da Nang Air Base. (Excerpted from vspa.com)

[25] The only English-language newspaper readily available was the "Stars and Stripes", a military publication that was distributed weekly. Sometimes our families would send magazines and newspapers from home, but our only regular source of news was the "Stars and Stripes".

barracks that had taken many rocket rounds and incurred many casualties. He explained how he met two hospitalized soldiers and that they had taught him how we must care for each other. They were in their hospital beds unable to take cover when the attack had begun. They had no choice but to stay in their beds, exposed to the dangers of shrapnel during the attack. Terrified, they had comforted each other by pulling and rolling their beds as near as possible and touching their bare toes together. Their simple act of touch let each know that the other was OK and that neither was alone in their terror. They had managed through the attack without further injury. They were soon to be evacuated to Japan for further medical care. We listened to this story of terror, friendship, and caring and we thanked our lucky stars that, although our own lives had been threatened, we had at least been able to take cover. We'd just heard a story about true courage. Each of us wondered if we could garner that same courage the next time we came under fire.

CHAPTER 11 - ZEKE AND CAMARADERIE

One of my friends in Company A, a fellow radio repairman, was great guy from Toledo, Ohio. His last name was a long Polish abomination of consonants that was unpronounceable by the average U.S. Army NCO. These sergeants couldn't be bothered with any effort to say the name correctly. My friend was therefore always called Zeke despite having his real last name clearly spelled out on his uniform.

Zeke was a charismatic wheeler-dealer with a wonderful sense of humor. He was the guy that got things done, legally or shadily. Zeke discovered that the abundance of bottles of hard alcohol within the Rice Paddy Inn of the 37th Signal Battalion could be traded to other military units in Da Nang for all sorts of great things. So with the cooperation of the NCO's that ran the Rice Paddy Inn, Zeke began prowling around Da Nang and making trades.

In May, Zeke managed to trade with the local marines He obtained a full case of New York steaks offering our Rice Paddy Inn alcohol in exchange. This led to the Company A barbecue I discussed earlier during which we ate steak sandwiches. They were delicious. Our normal mess hall food was just passable. Our milk and eggs were powdered and were reconstituted using the iodized water available. Both were awful. We rarely had fresh beef, lamb or pork. Our usual protein was chicken. We had it cooked in any number of unappetizing ways. Fresh fruits and vegetables were also uncommon and desserts consisted of Jell-O, cakes and cookies. God bless Zeke for finding New York steaks.

Zeke discovered that we could eat at the Air Force mess hall located just a few blocks from our compound. All we had to do was walk there and sign in as Army visitors. We were welcome at the Air Force mess as long as we did not abuse the privilege by over-using the facility. This was a great thing. The Air Force operated transports that flew real food into Da Nang. Their mess had real milk, real eggs, fresh fruits and, Lord oh Lord, ice cream. So we occasionally trekked over to the Air Force and indulged ourselves in their abundance of fresh foods.

In early August Zeke made friends with the Air Force's local HAM radio operator. By trading alcohol, I am fairly certain, he arranged for the two of us to use that facility to phone home. We stayed up after our working shift and showed up at the Air Force radio station at 2 in the morning, four in the afternoon California time. Zeke's Air Force friend sat us down at the HAM station and explained to us how it operated. Zeke was first. The operator asked for his home phone number in the United States and then set up a chain or radio connections followed by a telephone connection. The phone at Zeke's mother's home rang. Ham radios operate on a single side band. This means that communications are one-way and one person at a time speaks. When one person finishes speaking, he or she must say "over" allowing the radio operators to shift communications from one direction to the other. Zeke's mother answered the phone and Zeke said "Hi Mom. How are you?" His mother immediately began crying. Poor Zeke could only say, "Oh shit, Mom" and then he hung up. How sad and well, what else could he do?

Now it was my turn. I gave the operator Lauren's home phone number and that line rang. I discovered that Lauren was baby-sitting and her mom gave the operator that phone number. When she answered all I could say was, "Hello, I love you. Over". To which she replied, "I love you too. Over". All along the path of communications various HAM radio operators were listening to our conversation so that they could make signal switches when they heard the handoff word "over". This was very awkward. There was so much more I wanted to say but all we could do was offer loving platitudes. At least Lauren knew I was well and could pass this information on to my family. I was grateful for the call even though it was uncomfortable and far less than private.

Zeke and I remained friends when we returned home to the states. Lauren and I visited him in Toledo when I was discharged from the Army in 1969. Over the years time and distance caused us to lose touch with each other. I will forever remember his humor, outgoing personality and gracious ability to share his talents.

My other friends were from New Jersey, Texas, Massachusetts and North Carolina. I became familiar with multiple American accents, sayings and culture. I learned that 'oil', 'all', and 'earl' were all the same sticky slick lubricant and that 'tire' and 'tar' were the exact same rubber sphere that went around a wheel rim. I learned that Bostonians asked that a beer be drawn, Californians asked for a beer to be poured, and Texans said, "Get me a fucking beer".

We lived together in relatively close quarters. We endured attacks together. We worked, ate, drank and partied together. We had families to whom we wrote and from whom we received letters and care packages filled with candies, cookies and other sweets from home. We shared the contents of the care packages. We had girl friends that wrote to us and for whom we returned letters of love and longing. We teased each other and supported each other. Given the opportunity of circumstance, each of us would have given his life for the other. This level of camaraderie is difficult to explain to those who have never operated as a part of a team, away from their homes in dangerous situations, and with a mission. I became most aware of the camaraderie I had experienced when I left Viet Nam to return home; alone and without the companionship of my military colleagues.

CHAPTER 12 - QUI NHON

Eventually I became bored with my weekly routine. I repaired radios at night, wrote letters between 0200 and 0400, slept from 0400 until 1100, worked in the N.C.O. club from noon until 0500, ate dinner and repeated the same activities day in and day out. On weekends I would catch up on my sleep, walk to the base exchange, go to the local movie, drink at the Rice Paddy Inn, or head for China Beach. I was confined to the area of the air base and I needed a break from the routine. It came from out of the blue from the officer in charge of the maintenance lab.

My maintenance lab officer assigned me the duty of transporting two large pallets of old electronic equipment from Da Nang to Qui Nhon to be exchanged for new equipment. I loaded four large radios and a number of multiplexor modems into a truck and went to the air base. Then I loaded the equipment and myself onto a Canadian made Otter fixed wing aircraft. The plane took off over Da Nang and began a southerly flight to Qui Nhon. The view was spectacular. The C-130 and C-141 aircraft I had previously flown on had had no windows. This was my first view of Viet Nam from the air.

The Viet Nam I saw from the air was spectacularly green. It was covered with shades that ran from the deep, fresh and very bright green of newly grown rice to the dark forest green of the mountainous jungles. The green land was strewn with ribbons of water created by the rivers that drained the wet mountains in the west. As the rivers neared the South China Sea their deltas extended fingers of water in multiple spokes toward the ocean. The land began at the shores of the South China Sea and extended westward in a flat piedmont that eventually ended with the sharp peaks of the country's inland mountain ranges. The mountains were jagged, picturesque and haunting in appearance. From the air, Viet Nam was a splendidly beautiful place.

The Otter landed at Qui Nhon and I unloaded the electronic equipment. I reloaded it onto a truck and the equipment and I traveled west to another signal base where the exchange would occur. This base was located in a drier hilly area just west of Qui Nhon. Its buildings were two-story wooden structures and seemed more permanent than those in Da Nang. This base was also further away from the populated areas of Qui Nhon and seemed more exposed to the possibility of attack by the Viet Cong. Although it was daylight, I was more nervous than usual. I entered one of the buildings and was escorted upstairs to the second floor where I was told to wait. While I was waiting I heard a considerable amount of yelling outside. The yells were panicked and I became immediately alert and concerned. I looked out the wide-open window and saw six or seven soldiers running in all directions. They were yelling "snake, snake". Not far from the direction from which they had fled I saw the snake. Its body was about one foot in diameter and it was heading up the small hill next to the building I was in at an alarming speed (perhaps ten miles an hour). The snake was configured in a series of concatenated "s" shapes like a long regularly squiggled line. It was moving in a direction of about 45 degrees to the right of the line formed from its head to its tail (The continuous "s" shapes of its body were superimposed along that line; So it seemed to be gliding at an angle up the hillside). Its speed was amazing. Because of its "s" shaped configuration, I am uncertain exactly how long the snake was, but it had to have been at least twenty feet long when on-coiled. Its size and speed of movement made it a very impressive snake and I was very glad to be indoors and upstairs. The troops below me were terrified and might have faired better mentally had the V.C. attacked.

As it happens in the military, poor communication abounds. My efforts to exchange old equipment for new came to naught. The base near Qui Nhon where I had been sent to complete the exchange had no new equipment. I gathered up the old equipment, put it all back on the truck and headed home to Da Nang. About a week later I made a second attempt at exchanging the equipment. This time my transport south was by helicopter. The helicopter was located just south of Da Nang at Marble Mountain.

I was waiting for my ride at the side of the base road with my equipment for my truck ride to Marble Mountain. While I was waiting, another vehicle came along. Two medics climbed out. They asked where I was going and when they learned that I was headed to Qui Nhon, they handed me two boxes of whole human blood to take there. Yikes! Not only did I have a ton of electronic equipment, now I had human blood. They told me not to worry; I would be met by other medics when I landed at Qui Nhon. I caught my ride to the Marble Mountain helicopter pad and loaded myself and everything else onto a helicopter. The copter took off and headed south. I was seated behind the pilot and co-pilot.

The pilot sat in front of me with his hands on the collective, surrounded by the clear bubble of the chopper. We flew along for an hour or so and then a multiplicity of red lights began glowing on the control panel. The pilot said we were running out of gas. My unspoken response was, "I beg your pardon. What the hell do you mean we're running out of gas?" Then the pilot said, "We are going to have to land." Well, I thought, that's better than falling out of the sky. The pregnant question was: where are we going to land? We began a rapid descent, dropping below 1,000 feet and continuing down. The pilot was looking for a clear area to land. As he found one, the engine shut down. We were out of gas. Now I thought, "Holy Shit! What happens when a copter runs out of gas? Does it crash?" Fortunately, it was only a few hundred feet from a reasonable landing site and it "auto rotated" down to the ground. Enough centripetal force existed in the spinning blades overhead to allow the chopper to drop slowly and with some control. Had our altitude been higher we would most likely have crashed. OK, we dodged that bullet. Now my question was, "Where have we landed? Were we in enemy territory?" As our good luck would have it, we wound up in an area occupied by troops from the Republic of Korea. They found us in short order and within half an hour the pilots managed to locate fuel and fill the tanks of the helicopter. We took off for the balance of our journey - equipment, whole blood, shaken passenger and pilots - all happy to be back in the air, and thirsting for a cold beer at our final stop.

As predicted, two medics accepted the blood I carried when we landed. Because of our untimely landing in Korean territory, it was too late in the day to travel west. So I went to another signal company in Qui Nhon and found a bunk for the night. The next morning I headed west again to exchange the equipment. This time I was successful and before noon I was back on another helicopter with new equipment heading north toward Da Nang.

The helicopter I was on was the classic Bell UH-1 "Hueys". During the war, the skies of Viet Nam were filled with these helicopters, but this was my first time riding in one. The crew of the helicopter included a door gunner. He sat in the open door, a door whose contours curved down and encroached into part of the floor. The gunner, and some of the passengers, could look down through the door's encroachment to the land below. This improved the range of motion of the door gun, but it also increased one's sense of height. I found it unnerving. Once again, I enjoyed the spectacular view of Viet Nam from the air. The copter flew over the coastline for a short excursion over the South China Sea. The door gunner wanted to test his weapons. Once over the ocean, he fired several short bursts from his machine gun. The gun's sounds were diminished by the constant noise of the helicopter and had I not been watching, I might not have known that the guns had fired.

As we approached Marble Mountain for our landing, the pilot banked the chopper into a circular trajectory and we spun down toward the chopper pad. This steep banked angle of flight and our tight circular flight path caused me to lose the horizon and all sense of up, down, right, left, forward or backward. My head was spinning and my sense of balance reeled out of control. My brain screamed for stability. The stability I sought reclaimed my senses a few seconds after we were stopped on the ground. I stumbled off the chopper and away from its landing pad. I'd had

enough adventure and the boring routine of Da Nang
sounded very good to me.

CHAPTER 13 - THE WATER TOWER

Our Battalion was divided into four companies. Companies A and HQ (Headquarters) were both located in Da Nang within our compound. Company B operated to our North in Dong Ha, Hue, and Quang Tri; while Company C operated to our south in Hoi An, Chu Lai and Tam Ky. Each line company was commanded by an officer with the rank of captain or higher.

In June a new commander took charge of my Company, Company A. [26] He was a West Point graduate, a captain and fresh from the stateside army. He was ready to take charge and mold Company A to his standards. Unfortunately, his standards included far more of the spit and polish associated with stateside duty than my Da Nang colleagues and I liked. We were soldiers and could tolerate the familiar stateside bullshit: neat uniforms, polished boots, hats at all times, and clean barracks. Unfortunately, the West Point military standards of our commanding officer extended beyond individual military appearance to the appearance of our compound, especially to our buildings.

Our buildings were simply constructed white stucco structures with corrugated metal roofs. They had been built by the French and were configured in neat military rows. Our commander decided that they needed paint. Not just any paint would do, however. Our West Point commander had us paint the barracks, the mess hall and the company headquarters building with orange and white checks. The orange he selected was Signal Corps Orange, a very bright

---

[26] For reasons I never understood, most enlisted men served yearlong tours in Viet Nam, while most officers served only six months.

almost electric color. Work parties were assembled and they began painting each building with large checks in "checker board" fashion. One large four-foot check of white was painted next to another large four-foot check of Signal Corps Orange and so on until each building was covered. I suppose the results were impressive. Once painted, our compound looked very military, very official and with its highflying antennas and orange colors, distinctively Signal Corps. This would have been great had we been in the states.

Now, please consider the thinking of those of us who had been in Da Nang for six or seven months. We had been rocketed at least four times. We had taken casualties. We were right next to the air base runway. Our compound contained two 30 to 40 foot tall topographic antennas and dozens of microwave and high frequency radio antennas. We were a key communications facility for the entire Da Nang area. We were amid a key enemy target. All that was missing was a bull's eye. Now let's mix in a gung-ho West Point graduate with a propensity for appearance. Why not paint all the buildings with Signal Corps Orange and White checks? Well, OK, what the hay? You could already find us as a nighttime target by sighting in on our antennas. You couldn't see most of our buildings at night. So what if they were colorful? But wait! The painting didn't stop with our buildings. Our company commander had us paint orange and white checks on our forty-foot tall water tower. Now we had the bull's eye.

The water tower stood just inside the main gate of the compound along its western edge just inside its barbed wire fence. It was about forty feet in total height and was constructed using heavy wooden timbers. A round covered tank sat on a platform some thirty feet above the ground and contained the water used for our shower, toilet and kitchen facilities. Our barracks, headquarters buildings, mess hall and communications facilities were located between the water tower and the huge topographic antennas on the other side of the compound. Bull's eye!

Now here's a probable attack situation: It's 0300 hours and the enemy would like to rocket the air base. Oh, look! See that forty-foot tower with the orange and white checks? Aim just below that tower and those antennas. Fire a few rockets for effect. Good shot! Now aim just the other side of the same tower. Nice shot! You hit the air base runway. Let's get out of here.

Needless to say, the morale of our company was immediately diminished by the orange checks on the water tower. Frequent company conversations asserted that West Point did not teach its officers much in the way of common sense. Good grief! Was our company commander nuts? I was personally insulted by the stupidity of his painted water tower. I have always been a very quiet, unassuming and obedient person. I've never been one to talk back, openly question authority, argue or mouth off. For heaven's sake, I had been an altar boy and a boy scout. Well, this was very different and this time I had to do something.

I worked the swing shift and benefited from an absence of officers and a diminished number of non-commissioned officers. They all operated during the day. I spent the end of one of my shifts in the back room of the maintenance lab making signs. I had gone to the U.S.O. during the day and purchased several large pieces of art paper and a box of colored chalk. I took these materials and made two-foot by four-foot signs with orange and white checkerboard backgrounds. The signs read: *Corn Chex, Rice Chex, Wheat Chex,* and *Checker Board Square* just like the cereal boxes produced at the time by the Ralston Purina Company. At 0230 hours my friend Zeke and I went around the compound and posted the signs. We hung the "*Checker Board Square*" sign under the 37th Signal Battalion sign over the main gate to the compound. We put a "*Rice Chex*" sign on one barracks and a "*Wheat* Chex" sign on another. Then we put the "*Corn Chex*" sign over the door of the company commander's headquarters building. This building faced the company assembly area where we fell out every day for role call.

At 1100 hours the next morning our company commander assembled his troops in formation in front of the headquarters building. Everyone could clearly see the "*Corn Chex*" sign hanging over the headquarters-building door. There were quiet snickers within the ranks. I was nervous. The company commander was angry as hell. He turned to the sergeant in charge of the first platoon and asked him if he knew who had placed the signs around the compound. The platoon sergeant replied, "No sir". The commander asked the same question of the next platoon sergeant and received the same response. My platoon stood next in the formation. My platoon sergeant was the next to be questioned. Now I was really nervous and worried.

Platoon sergeants usually hold the rank of staff sergeant or sergeant first class. By the time they have achieved such rank, they've usually been in the service for five to ten years. They're usually savvy and experienced leaders. Good platoon sergeants know their troops and just about everything about them. Nothing slips unnoticed under their watch. There was little doubt in my mind that my platoon sergeant had learned of my previous night's mischief. Now the moment of truth would come and he would betray my behavior. Believe it or not, though, there is justice in the world and sometimes the good guys win.

The company commander pointed to the sign hanging over the headquarters door and then glared at my platoon sergeant and asked him, "Sergeant, do you know who posted these signs? My platoon sergeant responded, "No sir, I do not." Then, to my complete astonishment, he added, "but I think it's pretty funny, sir." A rumbling of concurring snickers rippled through the ranks. The company commander observed the snickers and stood silently mulling the situation over, then with what must have been some overall sense that he had foolishly overstepped the boundaries between stateside and war-zone leadership, he dismissed the company and stomped off into his office.

I will forever hold my platoon sergeant in the highest esteem. He, or perhaps he and several other sergeants, must have had a long conversation with the company commander, because several days later a small work party climbed the water tower and painted over the orange checks. The tower became a bit less obvious in the nighttime skyline and, more importantly, it lost its mystique as a symbol of ignorant authority. I learned two lifelong lessons: "trust those whom you know who work alongside you" and "never paint one of life's water towers".

CHAPTER 14 - ROCKET CITY

Just before 0100 hours in the morning on September 2nd nine rockets slammed into the Da Nang Air Base area. I and everyone else in my battalion executed our familiar defensive activities: We took cover on the floors next to the barrack's walls and covered ourselves with mattresses; when it was safe we traveled one-at-a-time to the armory, then to the battalion's perimeter and its bunkers; then we remained in position until the all clear. These activities were becoming routine. In fact, members of the 366th Tactical Fighter Wing, residing in their quarters just across the street from us, had named Da Nang "Rocket City". Although the attack involved only 9 rockets, the Viet Cong damaged 6 aircraft and wounded 8 people. They were improving their aim.

The first rockets were launched at Da Nang in February. This was the fourth rocket attack on the air base. Three more were to follow while I was in the country. For several reasons, the enemy found rockets to be their tactical weapon of choice. First, they were extremely portable: only two or three men were needed to transport them, set them in position and execute their launching. Most of the rockets used in Viet Nam were Russian-made and were carried down the Ho Chi Minh Trail[27] from North Viet Nam into the south. Second, the rockets didn't require special training or sophisticated equipment for their launching. They were fired from a lightweight tube that could be propped into place with boards, sandbags or any other stabilizing device. Their

---

[27] The Ho Chi Minh Trail was the name given to the jungle pathways used by the Viet Cong and North Vietnamese to transport supplies from North Viet Nam into South Viet Nam. The "trail" passed along a spine of jungle-covered mountains through Viet Nam and parts of Laos and Cambodia.

actual operation required the ignition of a fuse that was usually connected to a simple battery. Simultaneous launches could be achieved by connecting multiple rockets to a single battery. The enemy simply aimed the rocket tube in the desired direction and adjusted its angle for the approximate distance of the intended target. Once launched, the Viet Cong could quickly evacuate the launch area. Next, the rockets could be launched from a relatively safe distance from their target. They had an effective maximum range of 7,000 to 10,000 meters (four-and-a-half to six miles). The landed perimeter around Da Nang was semi-circular (the South China Sea bordered Da Nang to the West) so, assuming the enemy launched their rockets from as far away as possible to avoid detection, the four-and-a-half to six mile "rocket belt" around Da Nang was about 25 square miles in size. That was a lot of land area to patrol each night. Finally, the 140 mm and 120 mm rockets provided a hell of a lot of (pun intended) bang for the buck. They varied in length from about four to four-and-a-half feet and carried a warhead weighing up to 41 pounds. They were terrifying and they sent red-hot shrapnel flying in all directions when they exploded. Da Nang was the closest air base to the Ho Chi Minh Trail, the major pipeline supplying the rockets. The Trail provided a plentiful supply of rockets and the air base offered an attractive target. It was not surprising that Da Nang became "Rocket City".

Seven nights later, on September 9th, the Viet Cong attacked again. This time they launched just three rockets at the air base. But once again, their aim was improved. The three rockets damaged two aircraft, killed two people and wounded ten more. For those within range of the rockets, the continued attacks proved very frustrating. How could the Viet Cong continue to attack a major America base at will?

Rockets were a major concern for all of us in Da Nang. But we had other, more mundane annoyances: rats and mosquitoes. I became fully aware of the rodent population of Viet Nam while pulling guard duty one evening. I was in my assigned guard tower at 1800 hours, well before dusk. A small tract of Vietnamese houses lined the street directly in front of me across from my tower. The Vietnamese people in these homes were eating their evening meal. When they finished, they began cleaning up. They opened their back doors, which faced my tower, and scraped their table scraps off their dishes into the back alley below my guard tower. Dusk came and the small tract of homes quieted. The street was empty and lights came on in some of the houses. Just before full darkness I became aware of movement in the alley below me. I looked down and saw several small dogs eating the dinner scraps tossed out by the Vietnamese. I took a closer look. They weren't dogs. They were rats. They were the biggest rats I've ever seen. They were moving from back door to back door cleaning up the discarded food. Talk about an efficient garbage service!

Rats were also a problem in the battalion's barracks. My friends and I never left food out or about in the barracks, lest we attract a group of rats. Sometimes we set large rat traps (just like mouse traps but bigger) baited with food in an effort to kill the rats. Most of the time, though, they avoided the traps or set them off and ran away or, in one or two cases, got a tail or limb caught in the trap and ran off with it in tow (they were big rats). There was an ongoing myth about some enterprising troops that, having had their fill of rats, found a unique way to exterminate them. They determined that the rattraps were ineffective and that the rats should be shot using their M-14 rifles. Because this would be done at close range and because the barracks had concrete floors, the danger of a ricocheting bullet was huge. So these enterprising troops removed the lead projectiles from the bullets' brass housings, kept the gunpowder in the brass, and scooped waxy hand soap into the open housing. In effect, they created "soap bullets". At close range a "soap bullet" could easily kill a rat and it wouldn't ricochet off the concrete floor. Although this myth seems most plausible, I never saw anyone attempt to shoot a rat with a soap bullet. I also question the plausibility of a soldier sitting quietly in a barracks all night long waiting for a rat so he could shoot it. It sounded very unlikely.

Mosquitoes were also a problem. They could be extremely annoying at night, disrupting any attempts at sleep (or whatever substituted for "sleep" in "Rocket City"). One species of mosquito carried malaria. We were given huge marble-sized pills containing medicine to help prevent malaria. We were suppose to take one each day. The pills were so large and hard to swallow that no one took them. Why take a pill when an enemy rocket could kill you?

Malaria or not, the mosquitos were very annoying. To check them, each bunk had a mosquito net. When we first arrived in Da Nang we'd climb into bed and cover our mattress area with our mosquito netting. We'd carefully configure the netting so that no gaps existed. Then we'd doze off to sleep. However, if you needed to get out of bed in a hurry, the netting was problematic. During our second rocket attack I tried to jump out of my top bunk. As I leapt to exit the bunk, I became tangled in the net half way down the side of my upper bunk and wound up hanging like a fish in a net. This may sound humorous, but it was life-threatening. It greatly increased my exposure to shrapnel. None of us used our mosquito nets after the second rocket attack.

The rats and mosquitoes were annoying pests that we learned to tolerate. The Viet Cong rockets were intolerable devices of war that kept us ever fearful, vigilant and alert. We were in "Rocket City", home of raining rockets, rats and mosquitoes.

CHAPTER 15 - R & R AND HAWAII

Every soldier in Viet Nam was entitled to take a one-week vacation at some point during his or her tour. It was called R & R for Rest and Recuperation. Troops could choose a visit to Sydney, Australia; Kuala Lumpur, Malaysia; Tokyo, Japan; Bangkok, Thailand; Hong Kong; or Honolulu, Hawaii. Airfare and hotel costs were fully paid by the government.

My friends decided to visit Bangkok for their R and R. They had heard about the availability of Thai women in Bangkok and couldn't wait to go there to discover if the rumored sexual activities of that city were real. I chose to go to Hawaii but my scheduled trip there occurred after my friends' visit to Bangkok. They returned from their R & R. just as I was about to leave for Honolulu. They came back fully in lust with the "girl friends" they had acquainted themselves with in Bangkok. As soon as they got off their plane in Thailand, young women greeted them offering to be their friends. These young ladies immediately moved in with my friends in their hotels, and acted as both tour guides and consorts. Needless to say, my friends spent most of their R & R partying and having sexual intercourse. They came back to Da Nang claiming they were in love with the girls they met and, in some cases, even suggesting they would go back and marry them. They also returned with serious cases of gonorrhea, the symptoms of which took several days to develop and mitigated their loving feelings of affection. The city of Bangkok became known, as the place where you went to "Bang Cock".

I had chosen to go to Honolulu, Hawaii because I had imagined that I would meet my girl friend, Lauren there. We had discussed this possibility in the letters we wrote to each other. Of course, her parents would never let their 17-year old high school senior leave home to visit her U.S. Army boy friend in Honolulu, and they didn't. I left Da Nang in November bound for Honolulu with no hope of seeing Lauren.

I boarded a commercial airliner in Da Nang and flew toward Hawaii with one stop in Guam. En route to Guam my plane flew over Manila and I was able to look down and see the Bataan Peninsula, Corregidor and Manila Bay, the geographical locations of American and Philippine fighting during World War II. The plane flew on and landed in Guam. As it taxied toward the terminal it passed revetments contain B-52 strategic bombers, the very same ones that were bombing North Viet Nam. This was one of their home bases. I had never seen a B-52 and I was impressed by their size and their low, sleek wingspan. They appeared to be very formidable weapons. Surprisingly, their bombing in North Viet Nam only hardened the North Vietnamese government's resolve.

The airliner headed to Hawaii was filled with American troops. The majority of them were married and were going to Honolulu to be with their wives. I and a few others were the rare stag Hawaiian visitors. We flew through the night and landed in Honolulu at 3 in the morning. A light rain was falling and as we traveled by taxi from the airport to our hotel, we could not see much in the dark and rain. I shared a room with another soldier. We checked into the Outrigger Hotel on Waikiki beach and crashed into our beds. We awoke the next morning and opened our drapes to a spectacular view of Waikiki Beach and Diamond Head. The beauty of Hawaii dumbfounded me, and I immediately regretted that Lauren was not with me to share it.

That morning I telephoned home and spoke with both Lauren and my family. I had no choice but to charge the calls to my family's home phone. Both calls went on for quite a while and were difficult. My voice and safe condition were comforting to all, but my absence and the remaining four months I had in Viet Nam hung over the pleasures of voice-to-voice contact. I later learned that my Dad was very upset when he received the phone bill with the charges for my calls. He earned only $120 a week and my Mom worked to help support our family. I know the bill was in the tens of dollars.

I spent a wonderful week on Oahu. I swam and tried surfing at Waikiki. I visited Sea Life Park, the Punch Bowl and the other local sites. I took in a show by Don Ho at the famous Duke Kahanamoku's. He was a very patriotic man and his shows were filled with members of the armed services. He made a point of having us stand up for recognition during his show. I hung out most evening at a bar in the International Market place across from my hotel, and I drank my share of Hawaiian concoctions. Most of all, however, I rested. I was able to sleep through the night without the threat of attack and I was able to eat real food, not the powdered milk, powdered eggs and ubiquitous chicken of my Da Nang mess hall.

After an all too short week, I reluctantly returned to Da Nang. I was rested and that was a good thing. My remaining three-and-a-half months in Viet Nam would be difficult, both because I was increasingly homesick and ready to leave, and because the war was becoming more acutely active.

CHAPTER 16 - MERRY CHRISTMAS AND HAPPY NEW YEAR

The Christmas season arrived, but no one felt especially merry or jolly. The romantic thoughts of a snowy Christmas with Santa Claus and carolers were overcome by the hot climate and foreign nature of Da Nang. There was a war going on and it reminded us how far we were from home. Christmas had to take a back seat.

On the evening of December 21st our superiors gathered us and told us that "military intelligence" had captured a Viet Cong soldier carrying a message outlining an attack that was to take place that very night. According to the intelligence there was to be a ground attack of the air base that would be preceded by the launching of rockets. In order to thwart the success of the alleged attack the base commanders had developed a deceptive ploy. Just before midnight (the alleged time of the enemy attack) our troops would set off explosive charges along the air base runway. These explosions would lead the enemy to believe that their rocket attack had begun and that it was time for their ground units to attack the base. As the enemy units flooded the base in their attack, our guys (the Marines) would be waiting for them in full force and would destroy them. Detonation of the explosives, of course, ran the risk that the enemy would also launch real rockets at the air base. Therefore, we were to don our flack jackets and helmets, arm ourselves and wait in our barracks (on the floor next to the walls – under cover) for the attack to begin. That night we waited in our prone positions in our barracks, armed, in full battle readiness, unable to do anything but listen and wait fearfully for an attack. We heard the explosive charges as they erupted. The base intentionally set off its warning sirens. The exploding charges didn't sound at all like incoming or exploding rockets. Instead they made a muffled boom like dynamite loosening rock in a quarry. Several detonations occurred but nothing followed. No incoming rockets were heard chugging through the air. No small arms fire was heard. Nothing happened. We remained prone on the floor for another 20 minutes until the all clear was issued. Then, feeling foolish and duped, we took off our helmets, put our weapons away and went about normal nighttime activities. Some even went to sleep. It was just another night among many of alerts, fears and all clears.

I spent Christmas Eve drinking in the Rice Paddy Inn. I was very homesick. On Christmas day I opened the gifts that had been sent from home, ate Christmas dinner in the mess hall and called it a day.

New Year's Eve came a week later. At midnight many soldiers fired tracers and flares into the night sky, just as they had on the fourth of July. It was another impressive display of firepower, but it remained a stupid and dangerous activity. It was amazing that no one was killed. New Year's Day passed quietly. I had only six more weeks of my tour remaining. I hoped it would be a good new year[28].

The first week of the New Year began with a bang, literally. At four in the morning on January 3rd, rockets again traveled inbound toward the Da Nang Air Base. Again we scrambled

---

[28] Two good things did happen in 1968: I returned home and married Lauren. The other events of that year were horrid: The North Koreans captured the USS Pueblo; Martin Luther King, Jr., and Bobby Kennedy were assassinated; riots erupted at the Chicago Democratic convention; and President Lyndon Johnson announced he would not run for re-election.

to the floor of our barracks and huddled near its walls. Again the base siren screamed and again we ran for our rifles and took our defensive positions. Twenty aircraft were damaged and one was destroyed.

"Puff", the DC-3 aircraft that devastated the ground with Gatling gun fire, usually operated immediately after rocket attacks in an effort to destroy the enemy's rocket-launching locations. After the "all-clear" command, I decided that it would be a good time to capture a photograph of that aircraft. I found my camera and climbed up into one of the guard towers. Because the attack had just concluded, there were multiple flares in the night sky and more than the usual amount of distant gunfire could be heard. I'd always wanted "Puff to operate nearer to our battalion so I could capture a better time-lapse picture of it. I was in luck. Puff was out tonight and it was very close. I saw a flare drop nearby and then Puff opened up with its full fury placing a line of fire down to the ground with impressive efficiency. It was very close. I could hear the guns firing and I could even make out the outline of the aircraft in the darkness. I reached for my camera and set it for a long exposure. The camera took the picture. Then I realized that Puff was too damn close. I was standing fully exposed to any stray rounds that might head my way. I ducked down below the sandbags that lined the inside of the guard tower. Perhaps my imagination played tricks on me, perhaps not. I thought I heard several stray rounds whizz through the air near the guard tower. I thought, Holy shit, I must be a damn fool for trying to take a photograph this close to live fire. Puff operated nearby for several minutes more and then flew off to the south. I took a deep breath, climbed down from the guard tower and went to bed.

By mid-January I'd been in Viet Nam for eleven months. I'd been through 6 rocket attacks and multiple alerts. It wasn't at all surprising that I operated in a state of constant awareness. My sense of alertness was acute at night but the intensity occasioned by fear and danger doesn't turn off during the day. I was in a constant state of awareness both night and day.

As I was walking from my battalion to the Air Force mess hall for lunch while in this sensitive state of awareness, the air base siren began to wail. Though it rarely operated during daylight hours, the siren meant danger. It meant incoming enemy fire. It meant that I should take immediate cover. It meant that I was in mortal danger. I jumped into the nearest ditch and crawled into a corrugated metal culvert that extended under the driveway to the Air Force compound and allowed water in a ditch that surrounded the compound to flow unimpeded. I stooped down in the culvert and waited and listened. The siren wailed and then stopped. I heard no incoming rocket sounds or small arms fire. The sounds of normal base operations were all about me. Aircraft took off, jeeps passed by on the road and men walked over the road above me. I slowly climbed out of the culvert and up onto the road. An air force MP greeted me with laughter and an incredible look of shock. I'd taken cover in an open Vietnamese sewage ditch that ran alongside the compound's perimeter. I was covered up to my waist with a brown/grey sludge consisting of lord only knows what. While the MP laughed I began to smell the stench that emanated from my soaked lower body. A test of the base siren had been announced at some point just after I had left my own compound. I'd taken its sound as an authentic warning and had automatically ignored all normal behavior to take cover, even in a sewer. I didn't assess the nature of the cover I found other than it was low and under several protective feet of overhead earth. The term "any port in a storm" comes to mind. Within seconds of my appearance outside the sewer, laughing airmen surrounded me. They stood at a safe distance and laughed their asses off at the sight and stench of me. I turned back toward my battalion and slithered quickly on my way in humiliation. I couldn't wait to shower (with my clothes on at first) and soap up to remove the slime that adhered to me. It took several days for the stench to disappear. Although I was humiliated by it, my experience proved again that the human body sensitizes and "tunes" itself for its own protection.

CHAPTER 17 - HOI AN

In January, just after New Year's Day, our commander sought volunteers to accompany two fuel trucks from our base in Da Nang south to Hoi An, a smaller city that had one of our radio relay stations in operation. The volunteers, who would be gone about a week, would travel with the fuel and then help install a new relay station just east of Hoi An along the coast and in line with the stations that relayed signals north and south. A week away sounded pretty good to me so I signed up. I was due to go home in one month and I wanted to get out of "Rocket City".

A day later I dressed in full battle regalia (helmet, flack jacket, M-14 and ammunition), then climbed into the back of a two-and-a-half-ton truck, alongside eight 55-gallon drums of fuel, and headed south to Hoi An. Our small convoy consisted of a lead jeep and two trucks. All three vehicles travelled along Highway 1, a dusty road that connected the coastal cities of Viet Nam from north to south. Before our departure we were told what to do if we came under fire. The instructions were simple: get off the truck and away from the fuel, take cover and return fire in the direction of the fire being taken with as much speed and fire power as possible. The foolishness of volunteering and the pure idiocy of my situation suddenly struck me. I thought, "I must be out of my mind. I'm riding in the back of a truck full of volatile fuel through enemy territory. Our three lightly protected vehicles must be very juicy targets indeed." But it was too late for remorse and my only choice was to stick it out and pay attention.

Hoi An is about 40 miles south of Da Nang, so our small convoy drove south along Viet Nam's Highway 1. Highway 1 was a dusty, rarely paved, narrow two-way road that passed through small villages and rice paddies. It was hardly a highway. While traveling south our trucks had to stop to make way for a large battalion of the First Cavalry Division as it came up the highway heading north. It was an impressive parade of American military strength. Two-and-a half-ton truck after truck filled with troops and jeep after jeep moved along heading north. Multiple weapons were carried and/or mounted on jeeps, in the trucks and on various other vehicles. Overhead AH1-Cobra helicopters circled at low altitude seeking any signs of enemy activity and prepared to release their deadly armaments if necessary. The passing battalion rumbled with the sounds of rolling trucks and overhead helicopter rotors. We wondered where the First Cav was headed. No other Army units had yet entered I Corps. Years later I learned that General William Westmoreland was rearranging his troops in Viet Nam. He was convinced that the Viet Cong and the N.V.A. were about to launch a major attack at Khe San near the Demilitarized Zone. He had sent the First Cav to relieve the marines in I Corps and strengthen the area. It turned out he was very wrong. The First Cav wound up not in Khe San, but with the marines in the middle of the battle for Hue during the Tet Offensive that began a few weeks later.

The forty-mile ride to Hoi An seemed like a very long one and we arrived safely. I headed directly for the nearest beer. I spent the night in Hoi An and next morning we traveled a bit further south and met up with a troop Korean soldiers. They were encamped within a series of sandy, undulating humps in the land that were just a bit too firm and stable to be called sand dunes. The radio relay van and equipment we were to install was standing on top of one of the small dunes alongside the road. The next day it would be flown by helicopter to its site on the coast and we would go overland with some of the Koreans to meet it and set it up into full operation. We were 4 soldiers from my Signal Battalion and a company of ROK troops. The ROKs had been in this area for some time. Their camp was still primitive but they had the look of troops that had been in the field and on the move for a long time.

We had brought along a substantial cache of beer and soda. These were the two beverages of choice because of the horrid taste of treated water. Being in the Signal Corps, we had readily available trucks, jeeps and helicopters and we were able to easily transport both beverages. At the dinner hour we began opening our "C-rations" and we opened some beer. The ROK troops nearby looked longingly at our beer. We decided to share the cache with them and they agreed to cook rice (part of their rations) for us. Soon we had a small party underway, with beer flowing, white rice and "C-rations" cooking and international relations improving. The ROKs rations included canned kimchi, a fermented cabbage dish. In their rations with each can of kimchi was a small packet of spicy hot seasoning that was mixed with water to make a red-hot sauce, which was poured over the kimchi. The ROKs drank our beer and we ate their kimchi and rice. We noted the strength of the hot sauce and had some trouble eating it. We were not used to such a red-hot burning spice. The Koreans watched us eat the kimchi and sauce and laughed as we tried to tolerate the burning heat it generated in our mouths. They tolerated it very well. In a gesture of machismo for our benefit, one of them opened a packet of the dry seasoning and placed the entire contents into his mouth. Although he grimaced, he managed to swallow the entire packet. We all laughed and applauded. But, at this point it became obvious that we were all getting drunk and it was also getting dark.

Darkness, alcohol and a camp in enemy territory outside the guarded perimeters of a major base are not good combinations. Two additional factors complicated the situation: first, the kimchi and hot sauce we ate were burning holes in our digestive tracts. Second, we had managed to set up our small tents and sleeping bags directly under the trajectories of a battery of 105 mm Howitzer cannons. A long night was ahead. I grabbed my rifle and ammunition and placed it next to my sleeping bag. I reclined on top of the bag fully clothed and tried to sleep. My throat and stomach burned and I was a bit dizzy from too much beer. Shortly the battery of Howitzers commenced firing. They were perhaps 300 yards away and they fired their projectiles directly over us toward the coast. They were very loud and the rounds they launched could be heard whistling up and through the air. The four of us had a brief discussion about the likelihood of a "short round". We determined that the probability of a "short round" falling on us was low and further that we were all too woozy and ill from the kimchi to care very much anyway, thank you very much. So we stayed where we were under the cannon fire and suffered through the night. The cannons fired; the kimchi and beer regurgitated into my throat, the sand sifted into my clothing, and my head split with aching pain. I woke early in the morning well before daylight to find that the burning flow of kimchi had found its ultimate exit at the end of my tired body. I was literally burning at both ends. I spend the last few hours of darkness almost hoping that a short round would end my misery. The Howitzers fired all night ending, of course, at dawn when sleep wasn't possible. That night was one of the longest of my life, and I have a lifetime aversion to kimchi.

The next day presented another of the ironies of the Viet Nam War. My colleagues and I had been rocketed by the enemy and seen hundreds of examples of destruction caused by the enemy, but none of us had ever seen anyone whom we could identify as the enemy. Today we would observe more evidence that the enemy existed.

A helicopter arrived and lowered a hook that was attached to the straps supporting the radio relay van. The van was lifted off the ground and began its slow transport by helicopter to the coast. The four of us met with a group of Marine amphibious tractor operators. They had two amphibious tractors for our transport. Our trek to the coast would take us through some areas that were mined by the Viet Cong. Installed on the front of the lead tractor was a heavy rake-like set of steel claws. The claws were designed to plow the earth for mines as the vehicle moved forward. We were told that the second tractor would follow the first exactly in its path. We were to ride on top of the tractors, not inside, in order to lessen our injuries if a tractor hit a mine. Apparently the concussion and damage created inside this vehicle was more harmful than outside. So we rode on top at the rear of the tractor with our weapons in hand and our helmets and flack jackets firmly in place. Our instructions in the event of enemy fire were again simple: Dismount, take cover behind the tractor and return the fire with as much speed and fire power as possible. Off we went through the sandy terrain with rampant trepidation.

We moved very slowly as the lead tractor checked for mines. The ground was sandy and the foliage thin. Various grasses and small tropical trees grew in patches and clumps. Our ride was bumpy and it was hot. We were very alert and watched the distant trees and grasses for any signs of the enemy. There were sticks stuck like stakes into the sand along our route to the coast. Each stick had a small piece of paper attached to its top and rose above the ground at the precise height of the outside deck of the vehicles we rode upon. It would have been easy to grab one or more scraps of the papers on the sticks as we moved along our route, but we had been sharply warned not to do this. The sticks contained messages from the Viet Cong and many of them were booby-trapped with explosives. We avoided the sticks and notes like the plague.

Here along this sandy path of coastal plane was clear evidence of the enemy and his operation in this area. The Viet Cong were obviously real. But where were they? Who were they? What did they really look like? How did you find them (not that we wanted to)? How the heck did you fight them if you never saw them? Where did they go during the day? What were the Howitzers shooting at last night? With all our firepower and equipment, couldn't we annihilate this enemy? How could they manage to rocket us up in Da Nang night after night without being caught?

What kind of war was this anyway?

After several hours we reached the coast. A long, lovely beach with gentle surf greeted us. The radio relay van had been set in place by the helicopter and we began connecting it to its generator, setting up its equipment and propping up its microwave antennas. Just to prove to us that the vehicles we had arrived in were indeed amphibious, the tractor crews took both vehicles out into the surf and floated about for a few minutes. I suspect that they also looked forward to some fun after several hot hours of grinding through the sands. After their swim they began a return journey to Hoi An.

We spent two nights at the coastal site then traveled home to Da Nang by helicopter. I'd foolishly traveled with fuel in a war zone. I'd destroyed my stomach and swollen my head eating kimchi and drinking beer. I'd stupidly camped under the trajectories of a battery of Howitzers. I'd traveled through mine fields on an amphibious tank. I'd had enough adventure. I had just three weeks left in country and I prayed that they would be peaceful.

CHAPTER 18 - AN OVEREXTENDED TOUR

About a month before the end of my tour, five of the soldiers from my battalion signed on for an additional six months of duty in Viet Nam. There were some advantages to extending a tour: first, while in the war zone, military pay was at least sixty-five dollars more per month; second, if your discharge date from active service was a year or less away, it could be moved up to coincide with the end of your tour in Viet Nam[29]; finally, duty in Viet Nam was purposeful while state-side duty consisted of make work. Most of us were unimpressed with the idea of extending our tours. We wanted to get away from the heat, the rockets and the confining nature of our duties. We wanted to get back to the states to gaze upon American women, eat real hamburgers and enjoy the real world. We were surprised that five guys were willing to extend their time in the country.

For some months these five soldiers had practiced the recreational activity, if you could call it that, of traveling by jeep to a free-fire zone to fire their weapons. A free-fire zone was a designated location outside the perimeter of the air base where small arms and other weapons could be fired. Off these guys would go for several hours with their M-14 rifles and their ammunition. The routine of their activity was a deadly error. They traveled to the same location at the same time on the same day each week, thus establishing a pattern. Late one evening during the first month of their extended tours, we heard that all five had been killed. A remotely detonated bomb that had been buried in the roadway they traveled had destroyed their jeep. Expecting

---

[29] Those with less than six months of service time remaining following their Viet Nam tour were discharged early.

them, the Viet Cong had waited for their jeep and detonated the bomb as they rode over it. Had they not extended, they would have been home on leave with their families. Now they were dead. The irony of their deaths haunted us. Our battalion held a service for them. Five more names were added to the memorial that stood in the center of our battalion assembly area. I'd been in country for eleven months and the memorial now had twelve names, all of which had been added during my tour.

CHAPTER 19 - THE TET OFFENSIVE

General Westmoreland[30] announced a 36-hour cease-fire beginning at 1800 hours on January 29, 1968 so that the Vietnamese people could celebrate their new year (Tet). On that day, the eve of Tet, the masses of the Vietnamese people of Da Nang were roaming the streets and setting off thousands of celebratory firecrackers.

The din from the firecrackers could be heard as a low and steady roar, much like the sound of heavy surf beating the beaches on a not-too-distant shore. As the day progressed, the aroma of gunpowder pervaded my olfactory sense and its smoky residue hung like a tablecloth covering the streets and buildings. As dusk approached, Da Nang became suddenly calm and quiet. The streets, once filled with humanity, emptied quickly. People disappeared as though they had been simultaneously and instantly swallowed into holes right where they stood. The sudden absence of sound and the profound emptiness of the streets were frightening and ominous. The hanging smoke obscured all structural features and dampened the slightest sounds. From within the darkening evening and under the smoky mist, the world seemed frozen in time and space.

For months I had lived within 2,000 yards of the Da Nang Air Base and had listened to the constant roar of twin-engine F4 Phantom fighter jets as they took off in tandem with their after-burners glowing red-hot. Now, the Tet truce had placed a hold on their operations. Their noise was absent from Da Nang. The total silence caused by their absence,

---

[30] General William Westmoreland was the overall commander of the U.S. Forces in Viet Nam.

the disappearance of the people of Da Nang, the dampening effect of the evening, and the gunpowder mist were terrifying. Nighttime darkness overtook dusk. My buddies and I retreated to our barracks and attempted normal behavior, but we felt increasingly uneasy. Having never experienced Tet, we didn't know if the holiday was supposed to end abruptly at dusk, as it had. We commented on the silence and went through the motions of a normal evening. The silence remained and we eventually climbed into our bunks and tried to sleep. Sleep was never normal in Da Nang. After multiple rocket attacks, our bodies had become fully attuned to abnormal noises. Our sleep had become more of a resting of the muscles and rarely a resting of the mind. But now there was no noise at all. So, in our corrugated tin-roofed and screened windowed barracks, we closed our eyes, rested our muscles, and kept our bodies at the highest level of alertness.

The evening passed in slow, painful silence. Midnight approached bearing the awful hours of attack. Rockets, when we were attacked, always came between midnight and 4 a.m. Each of us, in our own manner, had learned to count the time from midnight until 4 a.m., knowing that a chance at real sleep would not begin until those hours had passed. Distant fire was heard just before midnight, but such sounds were not abnormal. As the time passed, we continued to hear more than the normal amount of distant fire. Then around 3:30 a.m. all hell broke loose as an initial barrage of thirty-six 122 mm rockets rained in and hit the nearby air base. The air base siren began its wail; the incoming rounds with their unique chugging rush could be heard followed by their explosions, small arms fire could be heard in the not-too-distant area. We fled from our barracks to the armory to retrieve our weapons and headed for our assigned defensive positions. The sky was on fire with flares and tracers.

Rocket attacks typically lasted several minutes. We always raced for our weapons and headed for our defensive positions when attacks began, provided, of course, that the rockets were not falling directly on our position. In the latter case, we waited for the shelling to stop before arming ourselves and taking our places along our perimeter. We would wait in our bunkers fully alert until an all clear was issued by the powers that be. Then we would return our weapons and go back to our normal duties. Most of the time the all clear was sounded within an hour of an attack. This time, during Tet, we waited in our bunkers and the all clear was not issued. We were in our bunkers when daylight arrived. We were in our bunkers all morning. The all clear was finally issued just before noon. While waiting we could here occasional small arms fire in the distance. We also heard outgoing artillery fire along with the usual heavy air traffic taking off and landing from the air base. It was most unusual to hear such fire during the daytime. Clearly something extraordinary was occurring.

As the day progressed rumors of enemy attacks and incursions in and around the air base trickled in. Sergeant A, who arrived from across the base, reported that position x had killed y number of Viet Cong who had attacked just after midnight. Specialist B, returning from his shift near Da Nang City reported that the Marines had repelled a company of Viet Cong. As more rumors found their way to us, it became clear that a well-organized attack had occurred. We were not making any discernable progress toward winning this war. From our perspective the situation was becoming increasingly more dangerous and hostile. Most of us had been in country for at least six months. I'd been in Da Nang nearly a full year. Over that time period I had experienced an increasing number of rocket attacks, attacks that our forces could not stop. Twelve names appeared on our Battalion memorial. Now, after a full year, the enemy was sufficiently emboldened and strong enough to mount a full-out attack on the Da Nang base. What was going on here?

What was going on was the Tet Offensive, an organized countrywide attack by the North Vietnamese Army and the Viet Cong, strategized and led by General Giap[31] and designed to cause an uprising of the people of South Viet Nam that would topple the South Vietnamese government and begin the ending of the war.

Because their communications with General Giap were difficult and uneven, the North Vietnamese Army (N.V.A.) and Viet Cong (V.C.) troops in I Corps attacked ahead of their counterparts further south. Saigon and the other major cities of the Second, Third and Fourth Corps were attacked some 12 hours after attacks began in Da Nang. Attacking enemy troops penetrated deep into the city of Saigon and reached but did not capture the American embassy. The enemy did capture the northern city of Hue. Heavy fighting continued there for many weeks until Hue was recaptured. During the weeks following Tet, American troops repelled the enemy at every location across Viet Nam. The N.V.A. and V.C. incurred heavy losses. Militarily, American armed forces were fully victorious, but politically Tet was an

---

[31] Four-star General Vo Nguyen Giap led Viet Nam's armies from their inception, in the 1940s, up to the moment of their triumphant entrance into Saigon in 1975. He was the leader of the North Vietnamese Army during the Viet Nam War.

American disaster. The offensive completely surprised the American government, the American people, and the American news media. Until Tet, all three groups had been told, and believed, that America was winning the Viet Nam War. Tet brought clarity to the reality of Viet Nam. It provided the American public with information that had become obvious to those of us in the war: the war did not have front lines; N.V.A. and V.C. forces could attack American bases at will; and despite the overwhelming superiority of the American military, it wasn't likely that the war could be won using the traditional methods of war.

Although not the military success as General Giap might have hoped for, the Tet Offensive was an absolute North Vietnamese political success. It changed American public opinion and began a long process that ultimately ended the war (although it took seven more years before it was all over). The Tet Offensive was the fulcrum over which the balance of American public support for the war fell to a grinding desire for disengagement. As I reflect back on that time, I am amazed that I witnessed one of history's historic turning points. Of course, I didn't recognize the significance of the Tet Offensive while it occurred. I grasped only the micro military meaning of the attack: the fact that things were not going well. As the years passed, I began to understand the macro meaning of Tet: that the war was not one that could be "won" politically and perhaps not even militarily.

I had less than two weeks remaining in country. I longed for home. I'd just been through another long night of rocket attacks followed by a long morning of alerts. Things were not looking good. Some of my friends who were also short (their remaining time in-country was short) began wearing their helmets and flack jackets and sleeping in the bunkers at night. I was tempted to do the same, but because I worked nights I found some middle ground. I went to my bunker after work at 0200 and stayed there in a half sleep until daylight. Then I returned to my barracks and slept until 1100 hours. I continued this "bunker to bunk" behavior until I left Da Nang.

CHAPTER 20 - DEPARTURE FROM VIET NAM
1968

I had only a month of duty remaining and I couldn't wait to get home. Many of us had placed charts titled FIG MO YOYO (which stood for Fuck It General - Mission Over - You're On Your Own) on the walls of the maintenance lab. We hung calendars below that heading and kept careful track of the days remaining until our departure dates. A few guys became superstitious about their remaining days. Having survived numerous rocket attacks and having learned of the deaths of the five soldiers who extended their tours, the superstitious began sleeping in bunkers at night. They didn't want to challenge their luck and wanted to get home whole and alive. With only a month remaining, I didn't initially subscribe to such superstitions, but that changed with the Tet Offensive.

Finally the day came for my departure from Da Nang. Most of my friends had returned home over the prior weeks and I really had no one to say goodbye to. A new group of soldiers had slowly taken the places of those that had gone home, and the Battalion was operating under their care. I loaded my duffel bag into a truck, climbed into the back, took a last look at the 37th Signal Battalion and left through the gate, another veteran done with Viet Nam. I went to the Da Nang base terminal and waited for my plane. As I walked to board my plane, I watched another aircraft as it unloaded a group of new troops. They walked, eyes agog, toward the terminal.

I flew south from Da Nang, once again on a C-130 transport aircraft, to Cam Rahn Bay on the South Vietnamese coast. I spent one night there in a daze while I was processed out of the country and dreamily anticipating my arrival home.

On the second day I boarded a commercial aircraft bound for Seattle, Washington. Nearly all the passengers were U.S. troops returning from the war. It was a celebratory flight. We were all delighted to be going home and relieved that we had survived the war. We sat in comfortable seats, ate wonderful airline food and drank alcoholic beverages. We enjoyed the courteous attention received from the flight attendants. They were the first group of American women we had seen in nearly a year. We were in heaven.

I don't remember the route of the flight; only that it was very long. A half hour or so before landing, the pilot announced that we were about to cross the coast of the United States. A serene silence came over the plane. All eyes looked out the window straining to see the coast appear. With reverence and appreciation, we silently gazed at our homeland. It was an emotional experience.

We landed at McChord Air Force Base, boarded busses and went on to Fort Lewis. We went to a processing center and checked in. We were given tickets to eat a free steak dinner provided by the local American Legion. While we waited nearby, workers began sewing new patches on new uniforms that we were to be issued when we returned from our meal.
Many of us simply skipped the steak, as we only wanted to be free of the military for a while. I phoned home to tell my parents my expected arrival time later that day at San Francisco International Airport. Then I walked about Fort Lewis in a daze. Amazingly, my new uniform was ready in a few hours' time. I went directly to the airport and flew home.

CHAPTER 21 - HOME

I am embarrassed that I don't remember who met me at the airport, but it must have been my mom and dad. I do remember walking through the airport terminal and wondering what had happened to the world. I'd been in the army for two years, isolated in boot camp at Fort Ord, California; then in signal training at Fort Gordon, Georgia; then in Viet Nam. While I was away, the country had changed culturally. San Francisco, in particular, had undergone a phenomenal change. The "summer of love" had taken place the past summer and a new group of young people called "hippies" had sprung up around the country. I immediately noticed a group of Hare Krishna followers dressed in yellow robes. Their heads were shaved and they were banging drums and chanting while they walked through the airport terminal. I wondered who the hell they were and what they were doing. I noticed that mini-skirts and knee-high boots had come into style. When I entered the army two years earlier, skirt lengths were two to three inches below the knees. I also noticed that men's hair lengths had changed. Civilian men my age had long hair and side burns. I stood out because of my short clean military haircut and my uniform. There were other uniformed members of the armed services moving about the airport to and from their assignments. As I walked along I had a slight sense that the public was avoiding me and the other soldiers. I was disoriented and a bit shocked at the new world I saw. More strangely, I didn't feel comfortable walking through the airport in my uniform.

I arrived at our family home feeling out of place. When I left a year earlier, I was many years younger in maturity and many years less appreciative of home and family. I was also exhausted. I weighted 135 pounds. An appropriate weight for my age would have been 165 or 170 pounds. My skin was tan from the persistent tropical sun. This was an amazing phenomenon given my fair complexion. I hadn't slept soundly in nearly a year. I had lost two teeth in Viet Nam rather that having them filled.

My world had grown larger and home seemed much smaller. The room I shared with my brother was exactly the same as it had been when I left, but now it seemed like a place where someone else, someone younger, had lived. My mother had knocked herself out to make home as perfect as possible for my return. I was welcomed with the royal treatment. Although I enjoyed the special attention, it made me uncomfortable.

Lauren came home from school an hour after my return. I met her in our driveway and she ran to me, slipped, and literally fell at my feet. I kissed her and hugged her. No hug or kiss has ever felt as wonderful, loving or rewarding.

Lauren was my anchor to the real world. We spend nearly all of our time together while I was home on leave. My high school friends had disappeared, blown by the winds of history to the ends of the earth. My senior class, the class of 1964, dispersed upon graduation to universities across the country, to Europe, to Canada (to avoid the draft) and inevitably to the counter cultures of the hippie era. Absent my friends, Lauren's friends were those whom I enjoyed. However, I found myself in the awkward position of older boyfriend (Lauren was 18 and I was 21) among younger high school seniors.

I was a Viet Nam veteran home on leave. There was no place for me in the longhaired, "summer of love world" most people my age had carved out for themselves. Although I enjoyed Lauren's friends, I was still older and in most ways far more mature than they were. There was no place for me in my parents' generation either. They'd grown up during World War II and had a culture far different from mine. In addition, and in concert with growing conversations throughout the country, I'd begun to question the wisdom of the Viet Nam War. My dad and many other people his age could not grasp the possibility that the U.S. had erred in beginning and continuing the war. For a while I tip toed around the growing debate over the war. Then, when I began to express my opinions, my dad grew angry and rational debate ceased. I was home, but I only felt "at home" when I was with Lauren. Without her, I would have been alone, trapped between generations.

In March I flew to my new assignment at Fort Bragg, North Carolina. I joined another signal unit, the 426th Signal Battalion. I was one of several returning Viet Nam veterans in the unit. The balance of the troops had not yet been to Viet Nam. Unfortunately there was not much to do. Most of the equipment used by the signal corps was in Viet Nam or in other countries. I had a full year remaining and it looked like it would be a very dull one. Soon I learned that my company had an opening for a company clerk. I wanted something meaningful to do so I applied and got the job. After a few weeks of typing morning reports and various letters, the typing of court-marshal and Article 15 (a lesser form of punishment) documents was added to my workload.

The typing of court-marshal documents was a sad activity. The court marshals usually began when a returning Viet Nam veteran joined our relatively inactive battalion. Stateside duty was filled with military spit and polish very unlike service in Viet Nam.

Returning veterans were used to a more relaxed military environment and took their orders from officers in the war zone with them. Back in the states, newly graduated second lieutenants and inexperienced first lieutenants endeavored to exercise their command skills on the experienced, skeptical and hardened returning veterans. This inevitably led to a veteran disobeying a lieutenant's order, often mouthing off to the officer with "fuck you". Implied in the epitaph was the feeling that "I've been in and survived a year in the war. There's nothing you can do that will hurt me." I saw this set of circumstances repeated over and over. The brig at Fort Bragg was filled with insubordinate returning veterans.

In March President Johnson announced that he would not run for re-election. His inability to bring the Viet Nam war to a suitable end was his primary reason for not re-running. The embarrassment of the January Tet Offensive had turned the tide of support against the war. Johnson was quickly losing popularity, and he chose to end his agony.

In April of 1968 Doctor Martin Luther King was assassinated and our battalion began training for urban riot control. This was especially odious training. We wore gas-masks, marched in a V formation with fixed bayonets and endured the humidity of North Carolina and the burning sting of tear gas. Fortunately we were never called to provide riot-control service. It was surreal that we would be training for the control of domestic violence having just returned from a foreign war. War protests were growing through out the nation. The political impact of the surprise Tet offensive some months earlier, along with Dr. King's assassination had set the nation upside-down. I was 22 years old and I began to genuinely question the nation's Viet Nam policy and its domestic political situation. The continued court-marshals I typed added to my concern and upset. In June of 1968 Robert F. Kennedy, the former attorney general and a candidate for president, was assassinated in Los Angeles. The year that had begun for me with the Tet Offensive was becoming a horrid one.

In early June I spoke with Lauren by telephone, and we agreed to be married. After her consultation with our parents, the date of August 10th was set. I applied for and was granted two weeks of leave to travel home for the wedding. It was a grand affair put on by both families. Close to two hundred people attended. We honeymooned in Carmel and then flew to Fayetteville, North Carolina, where I had rented a tiny second-story room above the garage of a single-family residence.

Lauren and I lived as newlyweds in Fayetteville. Our friends were other married couples our age whose husbands had been in Viet Nam. Strangely, we never discussed the war.

I was relieved and grateful to be honorably discharged from the Army in April of 1969. I had the feeling that I could now get on with my life, whatever it would be. I knew only that it would include Lauren. We decided to travel home by car and spend at least a month seeing the country. We stopped in Washington, D.C., visited my aunt and her family in New York, went to Niagara Falls, and spent a week in Chicago with Lauren's Aunt Mary and her family.

Mary was the head of the Chicago Women's Auxiliary of the American Legion. During our stay she led a group of women in a parade through one of Chicago's suburbs. Lauren and I watched from the side of the street and I felt tears forming in my eyes. I had been home in the states for 16 months and the civilian population had ignored and even shunned me. Now before me was a marching group of veterans and citizens parading with pride while others cheered from the street's sides. My emotions were worn. I hadn't realized how much I longed for someone to understand where I had been, what I had experienced and how I had changed. At the end of the parade, Lauren and I and her aunt Mary entered an American Legion club. Dear Aunt Mary immediately announced that she was with her niece and her husband, a returning Viet Nam war veteran. Before I could blink, the bar in front of me was lined up with a row of drinks, all for Lauren and me. I was overwhelmed and then, shortly, drunk.

Lauren and I returned to Corte Madera in late May of 1969. I returned to work at Pacific Gas and Electric filing drawings and later became a draftsman. Lauren took a job at the Pacific Telephone Company. Later I returned to college. I was a mature and motived student this time and I graduated in 1973. Lauren, who went back with me, graduated as a registered nurse in 1975.

In March of 1970 National Guard Troops in Ohio fired on, killed and wounded student war protestors at Kent Sate

114

University. The news consumed the media and horrified the nation. I was aghast and sickened. At this point in my life I was opposed to the war. I was twenty-three years old. The students were my age. How could this happen? Why were the National Guard Units armed? I remembered my acute nervous tension after my first rocket attack in Da Nang and how I would have shot the first Vietnamese person I saw had not my commanders calmed me and my fellow soldiers and ordered discipline. I remembered my riot training and how frustrating and tense riot control was. These were green National Guard troops. Who was in charge? What were they thinking? How did the country come to this? Why were American troops firing on and killing American students? What the hell was going on? If my wartime experiences had led to a distrust of my government, then this was beyond the pale. I was very upset and completely at adrift. Why would this war not leave me alone?

My brother Mark and Lauren's brother Michael turned 20 in 1973. They were of draft age. President Nixon had changed the draft by initiating the issuance of draft numbers. Each eligible draftee's name was drawn randomly and the order of the draw determined his draft number. Lower numbers were drafted first; higher ones much later, if ever, depending on the military's needs. I was livid. Seven years after my entry into the service and five years after my return from Viet Nam, the war had not ended. Worse, my little brother was now eligible for the draft. My questioning of the war grew to full opposition. Fortunately, both our brothers drew high numbers and avoided the draft. Nevertheless, the very idea of their being called to service was odious and outrageous.

Lauren's last year of nursing school took place at the Davis Monthan Hospital at Travis Air Force Base in Fairfield, California. She was studying there when refugees from Viet Nam and returning Viet Nam prisoners of war arrived for evaluation and treatment. The war was winding down and the North Vietnam government was freeing American prisoners. But the Republic of Viet Nam was unable to assume the burden of the war. Its Army of the Republic of Viet Nam (ARVN) forces were unable to withstand the continued and endless flow of troops and arms from the north. As the N.V.A. and Viet Cong began to take more and more territory, the flow of refugees increased. Many managed to come to the United States and passed through Travis Air Force Base.

It was a strange time. I was home, back in the United States, away from the war. I was married and owned a home in Fairfield. I was a computer systems engineer. Lauren was a budding registered nurse. Seven years ago I'd been in Viet Nam. Seven years later everything had changed. The N.V.A. and Viet Cong continued to advance on the cities of the Republic of Viet Nam. On Easter Sunday, March 30, 1975, Da Nang fell to the Viet Cong. I heard the news over my car radio on my way home from Sunday mass. Their flag was flying over Da Nang. I cried. I walked in the door of my house and fell into Lauren's arms and sobbed. Thirty short days later on April 30, 1975, Saigon surrendered to the North Vietnamese and the war was over. All my questions about the war and my time there, the death of my friends, the protests in the United States, rushed through me along with a heavy sense of loss. Loss perhaps not of the war, nor the loss of friends, but the loss of innocence and a time long past before I became a man.

I resolved to learn more about the Viet Nam war and America's involvement. I had to answer many questions and reconcile the war and its result with the inconsistencies offered by our government. I began reading all the books I could find about the war in which I had been so personally involved - and the war that colored the neutral base of my adulthood with its pigments and forever changed me.

PART II

In Search of Peace

CHAPTER 22 - REVISITING THE PAST

In April 2012 a rare set of circumstances occurred that allowed me to revisit my past. I was retired, and was financially secure, and as president-elect of my Rotary club I was expected to attend the Rotary International Convention in Bangkok, Thailand. In addition, I was and am a veteran of the Viet Nam War. Later that same month I found myself at 32,000 feet above sea level and about 300 miles west of Seattle, Washington, on a jet bound for Seoul, Korea, and then onward to Hanoi, Viet Nam. My wife Lauren and daughter Jeniece were with me.

Lauren convinced me that I should add a tour of Viet Nam to my planned travel to Bangkok. "Don't you want to see Viet Nam again?" she had asked.

"I don't know." I responded. I really wasn't certain how I felt about returning as multiple emotions arose within me. Why go back? The country smells bad and the climate is hot and humid. I had some unhappy memories. I had some normal memories; I even had a few happy memories. I was proud of my service in the army but I was ashamed of some of the things the United States did in Viet Nam. How would the Vietnamese people treat me? Could I handle the bad memories?

"Just go and find out." Lauren told me. "There is no point in flying to Bangkok for only a week. It's too far to travel and it costs too much money for only one week."

"OK", I responded. "I'll include Viet Nam if you go with me."

"Alright", she said. "Call Jeniece and see if she wants to go too."

Now I was stuck. Any doubts about returning to Viet Nam had to be placed on the back burner for a while. I had just committed to return and, as it turned out, my wife and daughter would be joining me.

As I began planning the trip, I started to assemble my thoughts and expectations. I was excited and worried, pleased and edgy. I was concerned about how I would respond to the revisiting of a war zone I left forty-four years ago. I was curious how my wife and daughter would respond to Viet Nam and its heat, humidity and alien nature.

Forty-four years earlier neither I nor any of my friends, family or fellow Americans would ever have imagined that I would one day fly by commercial jet from San Francisco to Seoul and then on to a peaceful, communist Hanoi. Wasn't Hanoi the capital of North Viet Nam during the war? Didn't the United States bomb Hanoi and Haiphong harbor? The answer, of course, was yes to both questions. I surmised that over forty-four years a great deal had changed. During my two-week visit, that last assumption would be confirmed many times over.

We flew on an Asiana Airlines Boeing 777. Asiana is a five-star airline and the service was wonderful. At 32,000 feet the ride over the North Pacific was smooth and comfortable. We flew through the day to the west toward Seoul following the sun, which never set during our flight. I ate a lovely meal and enjoyed a glass of white wine. Our flight path took us past Seattle and the panhandle of Alaska then just below the

Bering Sea. We passed Japan and then landed in Seoul, South Korea.

My first trip to Asia in 1967 was nothing like this one.

CHAPTER 23 - RETURN TO VIET NAM

An airline headset connected to an in-flight movie replaced the wax earplugs of my 1967 flight. The plane Lauren, Jeniece and I flew on had windows. The seats were comfortable. Our plane had air conditioning. We had blankets and pillows if we wanted them. I drank wine. I was not filled with the fear of impending doom, as I had been 44 years earlier. I was both amused and struck by the contrast between this flight of return and my first flight to Viet Nam and war. I clearly preferred this flight, but I could not forget the first one or my past feelings of fear, concern, homesickness and worry.

The flight attendants served us a meal. We could choose between a western or Asian meal. Lauren and Jeniece chose the Asian meal. It included Korean kimchi, a dish of fermented cabbage and spicy sauce. I had had my first experience with kimchi in Viet Nam, one I recalled with distaste. I eyed their kimchi but avoided it.

The Asiana Airlines magazine had a front-page headline that said "Da Nang, Timeless Adventure". I had spent a year in Da Nang during the war. I suppose that was a timeless adventure of a sort. Four decades later the term had a much more enthusiastic and happy meaning. The article advertised the vacationland pleasures of the cities of Hue and Hoi An as well as Da Nang. As I read the article my brain went into overdrive contrasting the past and present characteristics of war-torn versus modern Viet Nam.

Headed into war-torn Viet Nam on my first tour, my fellow soldiers and I flew through the night. We left Travis Air

Force Base somewhere around eleven in the evening, and we stopped in Alaska in the dark early morning, then stopped again in Japan as daylight arrived, and finally arrived in Viet Nam just after noon. Troop transport flights to Viet Nam during the war were timed so that landings occurred during the day to avoid the risks of nighttime guerrilla war. Four decades later my plane flew through the day and Lauren, Jeniece and I landed in Hanoi at night near eleven in the evening.

Our Asiana jet began its descent and I gazed out the window looking for the ground in an effort to time the moment of our landing. I saw lights and signs of modern civilization. Soon our aircraft touched down and we begin taxiing toward the Hanoi terminal.

The plane docked and the bell rang announcing our arrival. The usual bustle began aboard the aircraft as people stood and emptied the overhead compartments in preparation for their exit. The passengers were largely Vietnamese. I hadn't been among so many Vietnamese people in over 40 years. They were familiar to me. Their language is a single-syllable conglomeration of tones not unlike Mandarin. They are a gentle people. Rage does not suit them well and they rarely display their tempers. I had forgotten the soft beauty of the younger Vietnamese women with their slender figures and graceful clothing. I had forgotten the quietness of the Vietnamese men. The Vietnamese passengers scurried like modern westerners to gather their belongings and exit the aircraft. I assumed they were going home or returning to visit their families. They were in fact home.

I found myself once again a foreigner in a foreign country. I felt out of place. I was taller than the Vietnamese passengers. I was a bit overweight at 200 pounds and was no match for their slender bodies. At age sixty-five, I was older. Most of them seemed much younger. I am fair and white; while they were a lovely soft brown. I wondered if they were watching me and wondering who I was. Was I in the war? What harm did I cause them? Why was I in Hanoi? I asked myself the last two questions.

We exited the plane together - Lauren, Jeniece, several hundred Vietnamese and me. The nighttime air in Hanoi was hot, thick and very humid, and I broke into a sweat. The terminal was only mildly air-conditioned. We showed our passports and entry visas, collected our luggage and passed through customs. I expected a more robust scrutiny but it seems Viet Nam had not entered the complex world of the U.S. Transportation Security Administration. I found this ironic and a bit humorous. I had just entered a communist country. Implied with that adjective is a bounty of bureaucracy, authoritarian oversight and intrusive personal perusal. I found only a few uniformed clerks checking paperwork. There went one myth down the drain. Hooray for the other side. They've gotten this one right.

CHAPTER 24 - HANOI

We were met outside the airport's customs area by one of our tour guides, Mr. Huang, who was about 35 and spoke perfect English. He guided us to a waiting air-conditioned van. We entered the van grateful for the air-conditioning and headed away from the airport. There were no wire screens over the windows. There was no danger of hand grenades. The roads were empty but for an occasional motor scooter and a few cars. We traveled along a well-paved highway heading for the city of Hanoi. Huang told us that the Russian government helped build the highway and the bridge across the river into Hanoi. He reminded us kindly and without menace that all the bridges entering Hanoi were bombed and destroyed during the "American War". This to him was simply a fact and part of the history of Hanoi. He was, after all, a guide and his job was, in large part, the telling of history.

We passed several well-lighted factories. There were signs of a growing economy. Here were Canon, Panasonic, and Kawasaki, among other international names. We entered what seemed like a labyrinth of streets comprising the city of Hanoi. I remarked that I was happy to have not rented a car. I surely would have been lost on my own. The streets were well paved and we passed among many buildings and structures. As we entered the French quarter, Huang pointed to a distant building across a well-maintained garden behind a secured fence. "There", he indicated, "is the home of General Giap."

"Wow", I said, "Is he still alive?"

"Yes," answered Huang. "He is ninety one years old"

I was amazed. General Giap was the North Vietnamese Army general who defeated the French at Dien Ben Phu in 1954. He was the very same general that led the North Vietnamese Army and the Viet Cong against the American forces during the Viet Nam War. He was the engineer of the 1968 Tet Offensive that occurred during my time in the country. Although once my enemy, General Giap had, and still has, my respect. I was struck by the idea that I was in Hanoi at age 65 and my former enemy general was perhaps a thousand yards away and was 91 years of age. I wondered what it would be like to meet him. I would have loved to meet him. I would have loved to shake his hand and say, "You were my enemy once, but you always held my respect." Many of the generals in my army during my time in Viet Nam did not hold my respect, but you held mine and that of all your soldiers." How would he respond to that? I pondered this question, but I was only fantasizing. My mind and my emotions were running wild. It was late at night and I was tired from many hours of travel. The heat and humidity were beginning to take their toll. Was I losing it? No, I think not. My respect for General Giap as a military leader was real. Our van passed on through the French quarter to our hotel.

As we traveled in the van, I asked Huang how to say thank you in Vietnamese. He answered, "Cam On." This is pronounced 'gahm un'. Each of us practiced saying it several times. Interestingly this was a new Vietnamese word for me. I never learned it during a full year in the country. What little of the language I did learn was more or less slang. Now I began to understand the ignorance many of us had when we entered Viet Nam during the war. We didn't even learn how to say thank you, a basic verbalization of courtesy. Wow!

Forty-four years earlier, when I rode from Ton Son Nhut air base to my first base in Viet Nam, I passed through villages that were impoverished. Roads were unpaved. Buildings were thrown together, and sanitation was lacking. But on this trip Lauren, Jeniece and I saw factories and paved streets. Even late at night there were several dozen motor scooters running about loaded goods to be sold at the night market. The air was still hot, humid and heavy, but the stench I recalled form the past was gone. Modern advertising filled billboards and storefronts urging folks to buy modern fashions, beer, food and electronic products. There were still old Coca Cola signs sprinkled about but they were diluted by many other advertisements. Hanoi appeared to be a thriving city.

At last we reached our destination, the Swiss owned Hotel Saigon Movenpick, a deluxe hotel with doormen, air-conditioning, a world-class restaurant, pool, spa and many other amenities. We collected our bags, checked in and headed, dead tired, to our room for our first night in Viet Nam as a family. I put my head down on a soft pillow on a bed of clean linen sheets and fell immediately to sleep.

My family and I rose at mid morning. We headed downstairs to enjoy the hotel's wonderful buffet breakfast that included Western foods (eggs cooked to order, bacon, toast, juice, etc.), Japanese foods, Vietnamese foods and European foods. It was quite a display, and was a far cry from the powdered eggs and powdered milk I had eaten for breakfast many years ago.

Jeniece, Lauren and I ventured out of the hotel on our own for a long walk and some sightseeing before we joined our tour group later in the day. Hanoi was crowded and very busy. Thousands of motor scooters swarmed about the streets carrying passengers from place to place like busy transport bees. Many of the scooters were laden with goods headed to market. The drivers and their passengers wore helmets and dark glasses and their faces were fully covered by cloth garments to keep the sun away. The full effect gave them an extra-terrestrial appearance. It was dangerous crossing the street as too many scooters were traveling swiftly in multiple directions.

We had a map, but we got lost despite its assistance. Lauren stopped some young Vietnamese and asked for directions in English. They responded in English with considerable courtesy and they were very helpful. This was our first encounter with the local population and it was a positive one. My fears of being viewed as a former enemy warrior were diminished. In fact, the young folks that helped were born long after the war ended. Time is one of the kindest healers.

I observed the surrounding city of Hanoi. First, I noted, it doesn't stink. The foul smells of open sewers that I recalled from the past no longer existed. Second, there was substantial evidence of the modern worldwide economy. People had cell phones. Wireless Internet was advertised in the cafes. Modern goods and fashions were advertised in store windows and a wide range of electronic equipment was clearly available. Third, as we navigated our way through the city, I recognized a familiar characteristic from the past: the sidewalks and streets were perpetually interrupted by construction or repair. It was not possible to walk a full block without taking a detour around broken sidewalk paving, a pile of sand or bricks, or some other heaping pile of construction materials or debris. The sidewalks were uneven and one had to pay attention and walk carefully. All this was true in the cities of South Viet Nam in 1967 and it was true in Hanoi in 2012. Finally, I noted that the climate had not changed. We had been walking five minutes and I was soaked through from the heat and humidity. I remembered the climate from the past, but I had forgotten its discomfort. I could see that this tour would include many showers.

In the early afternoon of our first full day in Hanoi the other members of our tour group arrived. They had arrived during the morning from Los Angeles via Taipei. Our tour leader assembled us in the hotel lobby. We were all Rotarians or spouses and friends of Rotarians. There were 48 of us and we were divided into two groups of 24 each. Each group was loaded onto its own air-conditioned bus and we began a tour of Hanoi. Over the course of the next two or three weeks our group of twenty-four would get to know each other well.

One of our first tour stops was the Hilton, the infamous prison that held numerous American prisoners of war. During our bus ride to the Hanoi Hilton, I discovered that I was one of two Viet Nam War veterans on this tour. The other was a quiet, slender gentleman a few years older than I. He had served two tours in Viet Nam, both in Long Binh in the south, not far from Saigon. He had been in the Army Corps of Engineers and had overseen much of the work that created the infrastructure required for modern war. We Americans constructed many airbase runways; roads, bridges, buildings and other facilities that supported our efforts during the war. I didn't know how this fellow felt about our entry into the Hanoi Hilton. As for me, I was interested but anxious. I was not sure that I wanted a reminder of this component of the war. I was also curious to learn how our Vietnamese tour guide would explain this place.

Our guide was Nguyen Tran Trung. He told us to call him "Tom" and so we did. Tom was born in Hanoi in about 1970. He remembered the bombing that occurred as the United States attempted to intimidate the government of North Viet Nam into quitting the war. Tom was five years old when the bombing stopped and the war ended. His uncle was a North Vietnamese Army soldier who was killed while fighting in South Viet Nam. Tom was a Christian but also a follower of Buddha. This was a very non-western way of considering life and afterlife. Tom believed that his uncle kept watch over him. Tom was a gentle, well-educated man. His English was excellent and his English vocabulary was extraordinary considering that he had lived his entire live in Viet Nam. He learned much of his English by watching and listening to American television shows.

Tom explained that the Hanoi Hilton was but a shell of its former self. A brand-new hotel and shopping structure had been constructed on much of what were the original prison grounds. Few of the original buildings remained. They now contained some old prison artifacts including a guillotine and the leg irons and chains once used to lock prisoners to their beds.

The French had constructed the prison, and its architecture clearly demonstrated their influence. The words "Maison Centrale" (meaning central house) were painted in white

134

letters over the arched prison entrance. As we entered Tom explained that this prison first housed Vietnamese prisoners incarcerated by the French colonists. During World War II the French Vichy and the Japanese operated the prison and eventually it housed American pilots captured after having been shot down over North Viet Nam during what Tom called the American War.

As we toured the prison Tom offered us a brief version of his country's history and how the Hanoi Hilton reflected much of that history. The museum had displays showing how the French held their Vietnamese prisoners, then how the Vichy French/Japanese held their Vietnamese prisoners and finally how the Vietnamese held and treated American prisoners. The museum contained photographs of American prisoners including John McCain,[32] whose fighter was shot down over Hanoi and ditched in a nearby lake. Photographs in the prison showed the Americans being treated well. There were numerous pictures of their release near the end of the war.

I was surprised by the simplicity of the Hanoi Hilton. It was not overwhelming. I found that its most disturbing component was the guillotine used for executions. Any hints of the torture or mistreatment of American POWs paled to the staggering horror of the behemoth-killing device. The prison's displays told the tale of the imprisonment of many nationalities and the Americans were included as but one, albeit significant, group. The prison museum depicted the humanitarian treatment of the American prisoners. However, I was well aware of the many documented accounts of their

---

[32] John McCain is now a United States senator. He ran for president against President Obama in 2008.

torture. The displays were clearly biased but I was struck by their simplicity. They suggested that this prison had held Vietnamese, French, American and other prisoners. They suggested that the earlier prisoners were chained to their table-like beds and treated harshly but the later inhabitants, American prisoners, were treated well. Somehow the hatred and merciless madness of war had been lost. Only a well-used guillotine remained as a horrific representation of what the place had been.

As our bus traveled on, Tom recalled his memories of the bombing of Hanoi. He remembered hearing sirens and being rushed into a bomb shelter. Much of the bombing was directed at industry, power plants, bridges and transportation systems on the outskirts of the city. Bombing was not accurate in the sixties and seventies. Many bombs fell off target and killed innocent families. Tom said that after a while the bombing and the rush to the shelters became routine and a part of daily life. I can't imagine that!

The United States dropped seven million tons of bombs on Viet Nam. One third of them - two and one third million tons - were dropped on Hanoi and Haiphong. Three million Vietnamese died because of the "American War". Fifty-eight thousand Americans were killed in the war and many more on both sides were badly injured. Our first tour stop, the Hanoi Hilton, had reminded me of such statistics.

When we returned to our hotel, I found a copy of a Vietnamese-English newspaper. It contained an article announcing an annual fireworks competition to be held in Da Nang April 28th and 29th. It was an international competition and many thousands of tourists were expected to clog the city of Da Nang to observe the fine displays of pyrotechnic delight. I was horrified. I was under rocket fire many times during my tour in Da Nang. I grabbed our tour schedule hoping we would miss this event. To my relief, I discovered that we would depart the Da Nang area the day before the display.

I know what it is like to be under fire from overhead projectiles. To this day I can't tolerate being too near overhead Fourth of July fireworks. I tend to lower my body to the ground toward cover and I become very nervous and timid.

In 1967 and through February of 1968 I underwent many rocket attacks. In Hanoi in 2012 I empathized with Tom who, along with hundreds of thousands of Hanoi citizens, experienced their separate terrors from the bombs dropped by American B-52 bombers. I recalled how Tom remembered those bombings and I understood his memories and feelings. No one should have to experience such terror. Not Americans, not Vietnamese, not the lowliest of the earth's creatures. I was grateful that I would miss the International Da Nang Fireworks Competition.

At dinner a few nights later, I found myself in deep conservation with a fellow Rotarian. Our wives were in their own conversation but we were in a deep, intimate and very enjoyable discourse of our own. My companion, Lee was an English teacher, and we were discussing the books I read in high school and those he had his students reading. I remarked that I found Ernest Hemingway's description of being shelled in his novel *For Whom the Bell Tolls* as one of the most accurate I have ever read. We discussed the simplicity of Hemingway's prose then we discussed *The Great Gatsby*, *A*

Separate Peace, and other books. Then I told Lee how well Stephen Crane captured the beginnings of battle in his book, *The Red Badge of Courage*. He was never in battle, yet somehow he managed to accurately describe how a battle begins softly in a distant flank and progresses rapidly and terrifyingly into deadly chaos. Our conversation traveled in multiple and fascinating directions and I fully enjoyed every second of it. Later that night it occurred to me that my first new friend in Da Nang, the one whose watch was stolen and who was killed in our first rocket attack, was also named Lee. The irony was not lost on me. I hoped that my 1967 friend, Lee, rested in peace and that my new friend Lee and I might forever discuss literature and strive to find peace.

On day two of our tour our group boarded the bus and headed through Hanoi for a visit to the tomb of Ho Chi Minh. We approached the grounds of the seat of Viet Nam's government. Located there were the presidential palace, the offices of government and the resting place of Viet Nam's famous past leader, Ho Chi Minh. Large crowds were forming lines to visit Ho. He rested here embalmed under a glass cover for all to see. We passed through security and then moved slowly through a series of lines until we reached the entrance to the tomb. The crowd was quiet and there was a real sense of reverence. We were kept moving through the tomb and we passed Mr. Minh himself, lying in state. We were in the tomb for no more than 30 seconds. The experience was odd. We were viewing a famous man, now dead nearly 40 years. Each year his body is relocated to Russia where it is carefully maintained for its preservation. Those viewing the body were largely Vietnamese, but I saw many foreign tourists in the crowd. What did this man do to generate such long-term, reverent respect?

Outside the tomb, our guide, Tom, told us his version of the story of Ho Chi Minh. He was born in Viet Nam in 1890 into a well-educated family. His father was a government official. Ho was educated in Hue, Viet Nam. In 1912 he began traveling, first to New York and Boston where he worked at several menial jobs. He traveled and worked in England from 1919 to 1923 and then went to France, where he became familiar with the communist party and its doctrines, and began work opposing the French colonization of Viet Nam. From 1923 until 1941, Ho traveled and worked in the Soviet Union, China, Thailand and India. He continued his work toward removing the French from Viet Nam. In 1931 he was captured in Hong Kong and imprisoned for his anti-French political positions. Released from prison in 1933, Ho made his way to Milan, Italy, and then back into the Soviet Union. In 1938 he made his way to China and became an advisor to the Chinese Communist Armed Forces, the group that later forced Chiang Kai-Shek out of China. In 1941 he returned to Viet Nam where he led the Viet Minh (Vietnamese freedom fighters) against the Vichy French and Japanese, who occupied the country during World War II. The United States Office of Strategic Services[33] supported him closely, but clandestinely.

When World War II ended, Ho Chi Minh became Chairman of the Provisional Government (Premier of the Democratic Republic of Viet Nam) and issued a Proclamation of the Independence of the Democratic Republic of Viet Nam. For one year Viet Nam was a free republic. Unfortunately, no other country recognized its independence. During this short year of freedom, Ho repeatedly petitioned American President Harry S. Truman for American support for

---

[33] The forerunner of the Central Intelligence Agency.

Vietnamese independence. Truman never responded. Tom told us this bit of information emphasizing the irony of Ho Chi Minh's efforts to achieve Viet Nam's independence diplomatically with the help of the United States. This, of course, occurred many years before Ho Chi Minh's country fought the United States for the same purpose. Tom suggested that Ho Chi Minh's attempts to contact Truman were thwarted by the French who controlled all diplomatic and other communications and who wanted Viet Nam back in their own control.

Tom told us that Ho Chi Minh was a very shrewd politician and a man of many names, faces and political attachments. Tom also claimed that Ho was never really a communist, and that he was solely a Vietnamese freedom and unification patriot, choosing political affiliations as necessary to aid his cause. To prove his point, Tom cited Ho's affiliations with the country's last king, Bao Dai, and his siding with the west in his efforts to fight the French Vichy government and the Japanese. Tom then pointed out Ho's unsuccessful efforts to seek President Truman's assistance in gaining recognition of a free and independent Viet Nam. In 1945 the French returned and occupied Viet Nam. As explained in this book's prologue, Viet Nam and Ho Chi Minh came into conflict some twenty years later in a protracted war with the United States.

Tom also told us that most members of the Viet Cong were not communists. Rather, they were patriots fighting for the liberation and unification of Viet Nam. Their goal was to overthrow what they perceived to be a corrupt, wealthy, authoritarian government that neglected the poverty of the lower-class non-Christian majority and favored a wealthy, French-educated and largely Catholic upper class. Tom said that most members of the Viet Cong did not know the meaning of the word communist and were not members of the communist party.

Tom's explanation of Ho Chi Minh and Viet Nam's history may not be the one written in American history books, but many of Tom's facts were accurate, and his thoughts about the true nature of Ho Chi Minh and the Viet Cong (who were once my mortal enemy) rang true with me. I've read about the Viet Nam war extensively, searching for answers to questions that have haunted me since I was a soldier there. My reading has helped me to better understand how I wound up in the war. Tom's views of the war, of Ho Chi Minh, and of the Viet Cong synchronize with my studies. Tom helped solidify my understanding of what happened in his country. I saw the war through his eyes and the experience was confirming.

CHAPTER 25 - HANOI WAR MUSEUM

We left Ho Chi Minh's tomb and headed to the Hanoi war museum. We were most grateful for our air-conditioned bus that provided us with blessed relief from the ubiquitous and oppressive heat and humidity of Viet Nam. Unfortunately, the war museum we were about to visit had no air-conditioning. As we approached the grounds, various pieces of military equipment came into view. Here, spewed about in a random pattern, were helicopters, tanks, trucks, crashed aircraft and all sorts of artillery. There was also a collage-sculpture of randomly attached and stacked aircraft that had been shot down or crashed, recovered and brought here for display. It was impressive in its size and artistic assembly. It contained the massive, but often damaged, parts of F4-Phantom, F-111, C-47, C-130 and other American aircraft. Here for the North Vietnamese of Hanoi was a pile of the hard evidence of their "American War". And here, for me at least, was a statement of the wasteful and deadly technology of war. As powerful as America felt it was in the late 60's and early 70's, significant amounts of its military hardware wound up useless and defeated by the Vietnamese enemy.

The museum contained a series of separate indoor spaces, each one dedicated to one of Viet Nam's foreign conflicts. There was a section for the struggle against the Japanese, one for the struggle against the French, one for the "American War" and even one for conflicts against the Chinese. Many of us were struck by the seemingly diminished prominence of what we called the "Viet Nam War". As it turns out, the museum reflected the history of Viet Nam as a series of struggles. In the Vietnamese perspective the "American

War" was but one of several conflicts occurring in their history. Make no mistake, the war was a big deal for the Vietnamese, for me and for many members of my generation. It's still a big deal for me. Nevertheless, in the grand scheme of history, it was but one more of many conflicts performed on the world stage of political upheaval. It was also one more of several conflicts that successively aimed for the independence of Viet Nam. The war was presented in the museum in exactly that context. The museum's structure subtly normalized the significance of the Vietnam War by putting it in its proper historical position. It also seemed to diminish my year in the war to a very humbling degree. As I considered all of this, the word "waste" entered my mind. So did a sense of sadness and an offsetting gratefulness that my personal wastefulness was limited.

The war museum was our last stop on our Hanoi tour. We returned to our hotel and the comfort of our air-conditioned rooms. I was ready for a cold vodka tonic and a light dinner. We were weary from the heat and looked forward to the morning, when we would depart Hanoi for Ha Long Bay.

CHAPTER 26 - PEACE IN THE NORTH

No tour of Viet Nam should ever leave the traveler short of the experience of seeing and sailing through the wonders of Ha Long Bay. Departing the heat of Hanoi, we traveled north and east toward Haiphong. The countryside was flat and filled with rice paddies, water buffalo and small farms. Villages appeared and disappeared as we approached some northern coastal hills. The rapidly passing fences that surrounded some of the buildings along the way mesmerized me. They are everywhere in Viet Nam, and they have a certain standard arrangement or architecture. The posts are concrete or brick with some form of ornamented cap. Rails and stanchions are typically wrought iron or other metal. Although there is great variation, seeing even one of these fences assures one that he or she is in Viet Nam. They were there forty-four years ago and they were here when I returned. Neither time nor war had diminished their beauty or their existence and I found comfort in this.

Our route passed along roadways raised above the grade of the low-lying wetlands. The roads had elaborate, manually dug drainage systems. These were necessary given the heavy rainfall in this climate. We passed work yards containing piles of brick, sand, gravel, wooden poles, stone pavers and other construction materials. The countryside seemed to be in a perpetual state of repair and renewal. Villages contained an occasional hotel, many newer 4-story homes, and numerous street-side shops. The lower floors of village buildings were open to the street. Folks lingered in the shops and mingled along the narrow sidewalks between the shop fronts and the busy streets.

Soon we entered a more urban area. The number of hotels increased and we could tell we were nearing a vacation locale. We were just outside Haiphong, skirting the central city and weaving through its suburbs on our way to Ha Long Bay.

As we passed through the Haiphong suburbs, I was reminded that this busy port was mined and bombed during the war. It remained a busy port, but today it was a peaceful one. Our bus passed through an industrial area and parks near a deteriorating concrete quay. We climbed off the bus and walked down a steep bank, then onto a ramp leading to a rectangular launch, which carried us, 20 at a time, off into the harbor to board a steel hulled junk.

Over the next two days we enjoyed the comforts of the junk. It was a bit like being on a cruise ship, but it was much smaller. Our junk, one of several belonging to the Victory Star Cruise Company, had seen better days. It was old, but rather beautiful in its own way. It was one of but two junks in the area with steel hulls. There were many others made of wood and we were comforted that ours, as old as it seemed, would at least not sink due to rotting wood.

We sailed into the beauty of Ha Long Bay, a UNESCO World Heritage Site. The bay is filled with gorgeous tall peaks (islands) that seem to float randomly in the still waters of the bay. Most of them are limestone karsts created over eons of time. There are nearly 2,000 of them mysteriously piercing up through the surface of the bay's waters. They often seem to form linear bumps in the water like the ridges of some giant sea serpent. The bay's full name, Vinh Ha Long, means "descending dragon" and you could understand how this name came to apply to the bay. We discovered and visited several floating villages where small communities of people live and fish, or farm fish for a living. Their homes are built on piles near the shores of the many islands. We toured the villages and spent time exploring one of the caves hidden in one of the karst-like islands. Surely these islands and caves were used many times to harbor smuggled weapons, rebellious warriors, refugees and contraband. They exist in a complex labyrinth of water, land and mystery. It's wonderful that this area is now a World Heritage Site. Wars come and pass; yet the world has a way of preserving what is naturally important.

Our time in Ha Long Bay was peaceful, a respite from the hectic pace of our tour. We had time to swim, read, rest and reflect. We spent the night on the ship, but the room was small and dark and Lauren is claustrophobic. She wanted to sleep with the outside door to the deck wide open, so we spent our first un-air-conditioned night in Viet Nam. We were exposed to the full heat and humidity of the climate, and I recalled the heat and humidity of my many nights in Viet Nam forty-four years ago. I wondered how I survived. Then, I remembered that I worked my wartime job during the night shift from 6 p.m. until 2 a.m. and that slept from 4 a.m. until 9 or 10 in the morning. Rocket attacks and heat prevented sound sleep at any other time. Aboard a junk in 2012 I struggled through another night of heat and humidity, but the threat of a rocket attack did not exist. The war was long over and the bay was soothing and calm. In the morning we disembarked, climbed back on our busses and headed south to the airport for a flight to Hue.

In the evening we arrived at the Hanoi airport for a short flight to Hue. After landing in Hue we boarded yet another bus and traveled into the city. The drive to our hotel was a straight shot along a boulevard. The scenery was beautiful even though we viewed it through a filmy bus window at night. Our hotel, the Saigon Morin, was a classic French colonial structure. Our room was very large with high ceilings and spinning overhead fans. It was lovely and peaceful, but Hue wasn't always peaceful. It had been the site of a major urban battle during the 1968 Tet Offensive.

CHAPTER 27 - HUE

A highlight of Hue is the Citadel, the former palace of the king of Viet Nam. Our group spent several hours viewing this structure with its grand walls, moats, sculptures and nested buildings. The Citadel was the sight of fierce fighting during the Tet Offensive in February of 1968.

A local guide from Hue took us through the grounds and buildings. He discovered that I was a veteran and immediately volunteered that his father fought during the war in the Army of the Republic of Viet Nam. He opened his wallet and showed me a photograph of his dad, who was killed during the war. This guide was openly proud of his dad's military service and strived to share his pride with me. It occurred to me that doing so with the local Vietnamese, now under the authoritarian control of the "People's Government" was not an option for this fellow. I did my best to honor this man's father. The guide shook my hand and thanked me. I was reminded of my own sense of what it means to serve in the military and how such service might be honorable regardless of the political purposes of the government being served. It must be painful to find solace for service solely from foreign visitors.

Our tour left the citadel amid the torrid heat of the day. All of us were over-cooked and many were soaked through from the high humidity. We headed back to our fine hotel in our air-conditioned bus which was a comfort and a shelter. Most of us longed to take a dip in the spectacular courtyard pool.

I climbed into the refreshing waters of the pool with a dozen of my fellow travelers, and we swam and floated about. Up on the third floor of the hotel was an etching in the structure's stone that said "1901," the year that this fine hotel was built. One of my traveling colleagues asked no one in particular, "How did this hotel survive the war? Didn't the Viet Cong and NVA troops overrun Hue during Tet?"

His question was a fine one, but no one answered. Then I realized that I was the only one who knew the answer. "Most of the Viet Nam war was not fought in the cities." I volunteered. "It was fought in the countryside, in the mountains and in the jungles. Hue however was an exception. During the Tet Offensive, V.C. and NVA troops completely surprised the lightly manned American and A.R.V.N military installations in Hue. Some 10,000 enemy troops overtook and held most of the city including the Citadel. There was no immediate need, nor purpose, in destroying the building within the city. Rather, the communists sought to win over the civilian population and gain its support. The enemy held Hue for nearly five full weeks. U.S. military and A.R.V.N forces gradually retook the city, but it was done through vicious house-to-house street fighting. Many buildings and homes were destroyed or heavily damaged. During the war this hotel contained the University of Hue. It was initially taken and occupied by the Viet Cong and N.V.A. troops but won back a few days later by U.S. Marines. During the balance of the Tet fighting in Hue it housed refugees who managed to flee from the occupied balance of the city. Mortars, rockets and bullets damaged the building. It then became a refuge for those citizens of Hue who had managed to escape the conquered

---

34 The hotel is the Saigon Morin Hotel on Le Loi Street in Hue

part of the city. The hotel[34] was repaired and restored some ten or more years after the war."

Now another person asked me, "Were there hotels in Hue during the war?"

"Yes, there were hotels here and in other cities including Saigon. They were most likely filled with key political dignitaries from both the U.S. and the Republic of South Viet Nam, and the press as they worked and traveled during the war. They were also used by many American, Australian and other Pacific Rim civilians, all employed to support the war."

Now came the question, "Civilians?"

"Yes", I responded, "The war required the expertise and efforts of a myriad of American and other international corporations. They built runways, bridges, roads, communications systems, water treatment plants, buildings, harbors, barracks and tons of other infrastructure. Remember that at its peak, the U.S. had 543,000 troops here. They had to be fed, housed, supplied, transported and given bases from which to operate. A multitude of civilians helped provide such services."

"Oh my", said a traveler, "How did we get involved here in the first place?" The question came from a fellow traveler about my age. I was stunned. I was in the war. I witnessed one incredible year of it. I'd spent 40-plus years reading about it and trying to understand it. How could someone my age, an American, not know how we got involved in Viet Nam? I was hurt. My brain was struggling. Somehow I grasped that the war in which I fought was but a fleeting newsreel of memory to many Americans.   I took a deep breath and out flowed the wealth of knowledge attained from years or reading and studying the war.

I began by explaining the aftermath of World War II and the reappearance of the French in what was called French Indochina. As I talked, my colleagues assembled in front of me in the swimming pool. We were standing in waist-deep water to keep cool. I found myself giving a history lecture in a swimming pool. My class asked many questions and I took them one at a time and offered my best answers[35].

An hour and a half later I concluded. I was sunburned from standing in the pool, and I was very tired. My friends opened up a mind filled with knowledge and my thoughts erupted with authority upon them. I was pleased with myself for having helped explain how my country wound up fighting in Viet Nam. I was struck by the idea that if these travelers, my age, and in the country of Viet Nam, were vague in their understanding of the war, then many more Americans at home must also not grasp or understand the war. Then I wondered: why should they? Do I want them to understand because I was in the war and it's my need for understanding? But it was perhaps also true that a large part of me wanted the body politic, the people of the United States, to understand, so the errors of the Viet Nam War would not be repeated.

The questions of the day and the questions that I had tried to answer for many years had exhausted me. I retired to my hotel room.   My journey toward understanding would

---

[35] Please see the Prologue for my brief history of how the U.S. became involved in Viet Nam.

continue.   Our next stop was Da Nang, where I had
operated during the war.

CHAPTER 28 - DA NANG 2012

We took a boat ride on Hue's wonderful Huong (Perfume) River. It was humid but the breeze from the boat's movement kept us cool. The scenery was beautiful and peaceful. Our boat stopped at a Buddhist temple, a continuation of the peace of the river. Back on our bus, we headed south toward Da Nang. We stopped along the way for a seafood lunch at a waterside restaurant just north of the mountainous pass that guards Da Nang and its bay. I was anticipatory. We passed through small villages and saw rice drying on the tarmac along the side of the road. The bus approached the mountains that separated us from Da Nang, and then we began a long laborious climb up into the mountains.

During the war, the pass through these mountains was a key route for the movement of troops and equipment, and it was heavily guarded. Today it's serene and nearly empty of vehicles. Now there is a brand-new tunnel that cuts through the mountains allowing traffic to bypass the long, winding road over the pass. We were tourists, so our bus avoided the tunnel and we climbed the roadway up to its apex at "Cloudy Pass". We stopped at the top and got out of the bus. We were well-rewarded for the long climb.

I stood at the top of the pass and viewed Da Nang to the South and its harbor below me. I was numb. I saw a bright white city in the distance. There was a new suspension bridge. The city had grown in physical size. There were high-rise buildings. The smaller Da Nang I knew had been drab, grey and brown. No structure stood more that three stories.

I recognized the geography. There was Monkey Mountain, Marble Mountain, the river and the harbor. There was the airport and the airbase I once lived next to. It looked so familiar, yet so new and foreign. There was no war and I was close to tears. My daughter Jeniece stood with her arm around me while I pointed the landmarks out to her. My wife Lauren took photographs. I couldn't explain to them how I felt. I assumed my silence and my tears explained everything.

As our bus descended from the top of Cloudy Pass toward Da Nang my eyes were transfixed on the city as it emerged, bright and clean. There were numerous high-rise buildings. I located the airport, once Da Nang Airbase, alongside which I lived for a year. Off in the distance to the south was Marble Mountain. Many times I had looked in that direction during the night to see illuminating flares and gunships indicating the location of enemy troops. To the north was the City of Da Nang with a brand-new suspension bridge crossing the river. Further north, anchoring the peninsula of Da Nang, was Monkey Mountain. The geography was the same, but the city was very different. Gone were the dusty dirt roads and open sewers, the microbuses filled to overflowing with Vietnamese, the carts pulled by animals and the military vehicles. The streets were paved, the parks were green and well-manicured, and there were many commercial signs indicating that Da Nang was part of the world economy. There were flocks of motor scooters and motorbikes (as there are all over modern-day Viet Nam), but most astounding to me were the numerous new high-rise buildings. I had spent a year of my life here 44 long years ago during a war. As I viewed Da Nang from the top of Cloudy Pass, I realized that it was at peace.

CHAPTER 29 - HOI AN 2012

We did not stop in Da Nang. Instead, our tour bus passed out of the city and headed to a resort hotel in Hoi An about sixteen miles south along the coast. The road we traveled skirts the coast and China Beach and passes many modern resort hotels. Names like Marriott and Hilton appeared. It seemed foreign investment had been growing in Da Nang. The resort industry had discovered China Beach and its expansive white sandy beaches.

Eventually we reached our hotel, the Palm Beach Resort Hotel. It was luxurious and situated on the beach. Among its features were several restaurants, several bars, a wonderful swimming pool, an open-air lobby, and fine air-conditioned rooms. Delighted by the prospect of a brief respite for our hectic schedule, we stayed at the Palm Beach for three nights. The heat and humidity and our very busy touring schedule had sapped us, and we longed to lie on lounges by the pool or the sea and rest.

Ironically, I was in nearly this exact location in January of 1968, when there were no resorts and this area consisted of sand and a few scant trees and shrubs. The Viet Cong operated freely here, setting mines and booby traps in the sands between the coast and the city of Hoi An. A few days before my arrival they had overtaken the Hoi An Red Cross building and killed several German members of that organization. I was dumbfounded to find this place was now a world-class tourist destination.

After a day of relaxation at our resort hotel, our group headed into the city of Hoi An. During the war, Hoi An was little known nor worthy of much more than a stop along the road. Today, it's designated as a world heritage site because of its ancient buildings and structures. It's a very quaint and colorful town, still a fishing village, but now catering to the tourist trade. Its streets were filled with folks from Australia, Japan and other Pacific Rim countries. The city was filled with restaurants and shops, and there were hundreds of vendors selling all sorts of local goods. Members of our group purchased nicely tailored suits and dresses. Others bought custom-made shoes and other fine goods.

We enjoyed the respite of Ho An, but our demanding tour schedule required that we return to the Da Nang Airport. From there we would fly to Ho Chi Minh City, once called Saigon.

Our bus headed North into Da Nang and I craned my neck looking for familiar old buildings and landmarks. I wished that I had had time to find the site of the 37th Signal Battalion where I lived during the war, but I found no signs of it. The antennas that once made it a local landmark and an easy target for enemy rockets were long gone. I was told that there is nothing left from the war, and from the looks of the area this was absolutely true. Nevertheless, I kept looking and remembering.

CHAPTER 30 - DEPARTURE FROM DA NANG
2012

As a thousand memories whirled within me, our bus arrived at the Da Nang Airport. The brand-new terminal building was only one month old. It was modern and it contained a Burger King and other fast-food restaurants. Wow! It was a far cry from the old passenger/troop depot I remembered. Even odder, it wasn't busy. Once the busiest airport in the world, now only a handful of flights a day arrived and departed. This was once the busiest airport in the world. F-4 Phantom aircraft had taken off in tandem every few minutes, and C-130, C-141, Crusaders, and a multitude of other aircraft had fought for the runways. It had been noisy and hectic. Now it was peaceful. All of Da Nang was peaceful.

As our plane departed I peered out the window again looking for signs of the old Da Nang. I found none. I would not likely be back again, and I was happy to see this place in peace. I was sad that it and seen the face of war that killed many, ruined lives and harmed the land. In the end, I wondered if the outcome would have been different had the war not occurred. We did not win, yet this was a peaceful, thriving place. Was the war a waste? All obvious signs of it have been disposed. I was glad that I had returned here. I remembered the old Da Nang of war, considered the healing and understanding of time, saw the peace, and reconciled what happened. I concluded that the war had indeed been a waste.

CHAPTER 31 - SAIGON

The Viet Nam Airlines flight to Saigon (now called Ho Chi Minh City) allowed me to once again view the country from the air, something I had done so many years ago from military aircraft. I was again impressed by the beautiful shades of green shining from rice paddies, jungles and farmlands. Our plane approached Saigon and the rural villages and farmlands graduated into suburban and then urban landscapes. I had never been in Saigon during the war and I was surprised at its size. From the plane I could see main roads jammed with traffic of all sorts leading to and from the center of the city.

The Saigon airport was large and very busy. Major airlines from all over the world were represented at the facility's terminals. We landed and were whisked by bus to our hotel in downtown Saigon. Once again, the very modern and commercial nature of a Vietnamese city struck me. Luxurious hotels were abundant, as were shops, commercial enterprises and traffic. It was a bustling metropolis.

Our tour took us to the major sites: the cathedral, the post office (designed by Gustave Eiffel of Eiffel Tower fame), the central market and the like. On the following day we headed for the former Presidential Palace.

It was spring, and the parks and streets of Saigon were green and well shaded by lovely old trees. At the end of one of the many shaded avenues was the former Presidential Palace of the former Republic of Viet Nam. Today it is a state-run museum open to the public. It remains exactly as it was when it was taken over by the Viet Cong in 1975. It is being preserved as a monument to Viet Nam's freedom from U.S. occupation.

The palace is a fascinating piece of architecture, having been designed to allow for the flow of air and light throughout the structure. Thankfully, however, the building still had air conditioning.

We toured the various parts of the palace where the presidents of the Republic of Viet Nam had lived. Here was the site of many diplomatic missions and meetings held throughout the war. The conference rooms were pristine and had been untouched since the end of the war. American diplomats, generals, vice presidents and other politicians spent many hours within the walls of this building. Its grounds were expansive, lovely and well-maintained. Tall wrought iron fencing surrounded the building and its grounds. There was a large circular driveway that guided visitors to the front steps of the palace. The other end of the driveway's circular arc opened to the main gate of the grounds. This was the gate made famous by a photograph of a North Vietnamese Army tank crashing through it at the end of the war. We stood staring at the gate and the lovely grounds and remembered that photograph.

Standing at the seat of what was once the political power center of one side of the war was strange. Here were once the people that controlled the destiny of hundreds of thousands of troops and the lives of millions of Vietnamese. Their activities were little known to the rank-and-file soldiers operating in the country's rice paddies and jungles, and they were more familiar to those at home who followed the war on television and read about it in the press. The war was over. There was peace. The echoes of the voices of the old power structure had faded to near oblivion. Whatever they had to say then seemed no longer to matter. I decided that is important to remember the circumstances of the past, analyze the decisions of the past and make note of the lessons made clearer by the passing of time. It is good that this place has been preserved.

CHAPTER 32 - CU CHI TUNNELS

For some reason the tour companies in and around Saigon think that it's important that visitors tour the Cu Chi tunnels, and our tour was no different. We departed from our hotel in Saigon and headed west-north-west for an hour or so and arrived at the Cu Chi Tunnels, a venue that reminded me of a theme park. Here, surrounded by fencing and a main gate were the underground tunnels and living areas dug and used by the Viet Cong during the war. The place requires an entrance fee and has a large parking area, restaurants and souvenir shops. This was quite a surprise to a war veteran.

The tunnels existed right in the middle of an entire U.S. Army brigade. The Viet Cong occupied the tunnels, coming out only at night to spy and create havoc.

We proceeded into the tunnel area along clearly defined paths. Displayed were Viet Cong booby traps, pits filled with sharpened bamboo sticks, mannequins wearing typical Viet Cong outfits and carrying rifles and other equipment, and various artifacts recovered from the tunnels. We were walking in a thin forest. Trees and shrubs grew around the paths and the canopy let in an adequate amount of light. This was not thick jungle but you could only see fifty or so feet into the distance. Vietnamese tourists were walking about the area in small numbers and I felt a bit strange as I slowly walked through the area. I heard popping sounds off in the distance and immediately identified the noise as small automatic arms fire. I froze.

During the war, I spent all but two weeks of my time in Da Nang. I was not in the jungle on patrol. But distant small arms fire was a familiar Da Nang wartime sound. I stopped in my tracks, very nervous. My adrenalin increased, my listening became acute, and I looked toward the sound of the automatic weapon firing. One of the women in our group took my hand and asked me if I was all right. I was not, but I said, "Yes. I'm fine."

She looked at me and said, "No you're not."

I turned to my wife and said, "I have to go on ahead and find out what's going on."

She didn't understand and thought I was behaving badly. I quickly walked on ahead of our group in the direction of the weapon firing. I had to find its source to satisfy myself that all was well.

As it turned out, visitors to the Cu Chi Tunnels can purchase tickets to fire vintage weapons at a firing range that is part of the tunnel adventure. I found the firing range and saw several Vietnamese tourists gleefully firing away. I calmed, and then shook my head. Try to imagine my feelings. Forty-two years after the war, people visit one of its venues and actually fire weapons to gain some sense of the adventure of war. Huh?

I was annoyed that neither the tour guide nor the operators of the Cu Chi Tunnels warned me (or others) of the likelihood of hearing small arms discharging. The response of a Viet Nam Infantry Combat veteran would surely be more acute and reactive than mine.

166

CHAPTER 33 - SAIGON WAR MUSEUM

We had toured the presidential palace and we had paraded through the grounds and the insides of the Cu Chi Tunnels. Now we stopped inside the city of Saigon at the Saigon War Museum. Unlike the war museum in Hanoi, this one is dedicated entirely to the Viet Nam War.

The grounds outside the museum were filled with the larger implements of war: aircraft, helicopters, tanks, jeeps, trucks and all forms of ordnance. The majority of these items were American. There was very little that I could identify as once having belonged to the Viet Cong or N.V.A. It appeared that the object of the outside displays was to demonstrate the evil nature of the equipment used by the United States against its enemies, the V.C. and N.V.A. troops.

The displays inside the museum continued the theme of an evil United States military force. Rooms were dedicated to napalm and Agent Orange. Others were dedicated to American small arms, B-52 carpet-bombing, and the American home front's anti-war groups. The latter included the covers of American magazines (*Time, Life*) and headlines from American newspapers from the time of the war showing war protestors and screaming anti-war slogans. "Hey, hey LBJ: how many kids did you kill today?" jumped off one display board. I remembered that slogan well. I found it commonly chanted when I returned home from the war.

For me the entire experience of the museum was upsetting. It was a cold, hard slap in the face that brought the viewpoint of my former enemies into sharp focus. I walked about the place by myself feeling like a zombie.

I began my tour of this multi-story museum at the top and worked my way back downstairs. The final exhibit on the ground floor featured letters and artwork from the children of Viet Nam. Their theme was peace. Here at the bottom of a heap of depressing and horrid war artifacts and propaganda was a current statement of youthful peace. I broke down and cried softly. Thank you God, I thought, for the forgiveness and hope of children. I stood in a corner and let the tears flow. No one saw me. Not my wife and not my daughter.

CHAPTER 34 - MEKONG DELTA

We spend the last full day in Viet Nam touring part of the Mekong Delta. A two-hour bus ride took us southwest of Saigon, well into the delta. We crossed channels and small rivers and other arms of the Mekong River. The land was flat, wet, cultivated and green. The weather was hot and humid. As we moved deeper into the vastness of the delta, its enormity became increasingly evident. Cultivated fields, rice paddies, dark lines of thick tropical foliage and hundreds of fingers of water created a landscape colored in multiple shades of green, brown and blue.

Our destination was a small village on one of the delta's many small spits of land. Once there, we were fed a wonderful lunch of whole fried fish, tropical fruits and rice. Then we boarded san pans rowed by Vietnamese women and floated off along a narrow canal to a much larger channel of the Mekong River where we boarded a ferry back to our busses.

I was struck by the complexity of the delta. This land was not suited for traditional military battles. Only birds, fish, boats and helicopters could navigate across its complex maze of canals. It was obvious that many people could hide easily within its tropical foliage and along its muddy canal banks. It was also obvious that it was too vast and geographically unfriendly to ever be conquered and held. I wondered what our wartime generals were thinking when they entered this part

Here I found a part of Viet Nam that was completely unfamiliar to me during the war, a part of Viet Nam that juxtaposed the natural obstacles of nature and geography against the modern technologies of war. Here was evidence that technology could never have beaten nature. Why did we stay here for over ten years?

CHAPTER 35 - DEPARTURE FROM VIET NAM
2012

Lauren, Jeniece and I departed Viet Nam along with our touring colleagues at the end of April 2012. April 30th of that year marked the thirty-seventh anniversary of the end of the war. Our plane took off from Saigon heading for Seam Reap in Cambodia. I looked out the window at the flat delta as Saigon disappeared from view.

This was my second departure from Viet Nam. It was not as emotional as my first one. I had returned to discover how the war had changed this country and how it had changed me. After years of trying to understand the war and my roll in it, I had found some sense of peace.

The war for me was finally over. I was returning home to a familiar world, the world of 2012, not to the unfamiliar world to which I returned in 1968 after a year of absence and a generation of change. I was returning home to a welcoming world, not to one torn and polarized by war and unfriendly to soldiers.

My journey back to Viet Nam was one of discovery and one of affirmation. It solidified my thoughts about the Viet Nam war and about war in general. I found Viet Nam at peace, moving quickly into capitalism and world markets. I found parts of Viet Nam thriving with tourism, hotels and resorts and other parts teeming with industry. I found friendly Vietnamese people. I discovered the Vietnamese perspective of the war. I listened and I learned and I pondered. I tied my new knowledge to my prior experiences and all of my reading and research.

I came to some conclusions: The war was a mistake. Most wars are a mistake. America's intervention in Viet Nam probably made little difference to the people of Viet Nam over the long term of history. It was simply one of a series of many wars they experienced in their effort to be an independent country. In the long run it is, and will be, capitalism that wins the minds of the people and leads them and their hearts toward some concept of democracy. This will happen at their rate, and not ours.

At age 20 I followed my country's call to war, as had my ancestors before me. I was young, naïve and ignorant of the complexity of politics. I did my duty as was expected of me. I came of age in the middle of the Viet Nam war, and began to question my country's role in Viet Nam. I came home to political turmoil and many more questions. I read all I could in my effort to better understand the war. I learned that I am a person of peace, and that peace comes through understanding and service to humanity.

My return brought me understanding and peace. I pray that others will find the same without having to experience war.

Bibliography and Suggested Reading

Atkinson, Rick, *The Long Grey Line: The American Journey of West Point's Class of 1966,* October 27, 2009; New York, Holt Paperbacks - Henry Holt and Company, LLC

Bowden, Mark, *Hue 1968: A Turning Point of the American War in Vietnam,* June 6, 2017, New York, Grove Atlantic

Caputo, Phillip, *A Rumor of War: The Classic Vietnam Memoir (40th Anniversary Edition);* August 1, 2017, New York, Macmillian Publishing Group

Halberstam, David, *The Best and the Brightest,* October 26, 1993; New York, Ballantine Books, a division of Random House, Inc.

Sheehan, Neil, *A Bright Shining Lie: John Paul Vann and America in Vietnam,* September 19, 1989, New York, Random House, Inc.

Marlantes, Karl, *Matterhorn: A Novel of the Vietnam War,* May 10, 2001, New York, Atlantic Monthly Press

www.ingramcontent.com/pod-product-compliance
Lightning Source LLC
Chambersburg PA
CBHW071218090426
42736CB00014B/2875